In an era of shoddy and shallow political polls, there is one gold standard: the National Election Surveys from the University of Michigan. One of the nation's premier analysts of public opinion, David RePass, has found in their treasure trove of contemporary and historical data innovative and penetrating ways of using voters' own words to understand their motivations and election choices. *Listening to the American Voter* will go alongside the classic *The American Voter* as essential reading for all who study, do research and write about American elections and voters.

Norman Ornstein, *Resident Scholar, The American Enterprise Institute*

David RePass recognizes that the key to understanding voting is paying attention to how voters think about the election. Thus, in *Listening to the American Voter*, he uses the open-ended comments of ANES respondents to develop a model for measuring the importance of the attitudes that voters had in mind when making their decisions. RePass's creative examination of presidential voting yields significant new analysis of the 2016 election as well as fresh insights into the dynamics of elections past and future.

Herbert Weisberg, *Ohio State University (Emeritus)*

This work is a cornucopia of fresh, striking insights about how voters choose their presidential candidates. Employing quality data and several creative analytical techniques, RePass discovers the four key factors shaping presidential voting decisions: attitudes toward the major party candidates, issue concerns of the moment and party identification. Anyone seeking an explanation of presidential election results from 1960 through 2016 should read this book.

Steven Schier, *Carleton College*

Contemporary political behavior researchers have largely ignored a huge trove of data on the beliefs and preferences of the American public, namely, the vast reserve of answers to the open-ended survey questions in the American National Election Studies. Rather than force voters to shoehorn their positions and evaluations into fixed response categories, the open-ended questions allow them to respond in their own words. RePass carefully analyzes these data, showing what things mattered and how their importance varied over different elections, sometimes contradicting previous interpretations along the way. I hope that this welcome effort will motivate younger researchers to turn their attention to this too long ignored collection of data.

Morris P. Fiorina, *Stanford University and Senior Fellow, the Hoover Institution*

LISTENING TO THE AMERICAN VOTER

This book explains why elections from 1960 to 2016 came out the way they did. Why did voters choose one candidate over the other and what issues were they concerned with? The answer comes from talking to thousands of voters and analyzing their verbatim responses.

Traditional methods used by most political analysts have often led to false interpretations. The book presents a unique model that can predict the vote of 95 percent of respondents. The book also shows that there are two major forces—long-term and short-term—that can explain the overall results of an election. In addition, the author finds a new, highly reliable way to measure the ideological composition of the American electorate.

Appropriate for students of American government and informed citizens as well, this book is a revolution in the study of electoral behavior.

David E. RePass is Emeritus Professor of Political Science at the University of Connecticut and author of the landmark article "Issue Salience and Party Choice."

LISTENING TO THE AMERICAN VOTER

What Was On Voters' Minds in Presidential Elections, 1960 to 2016

David E. Repass

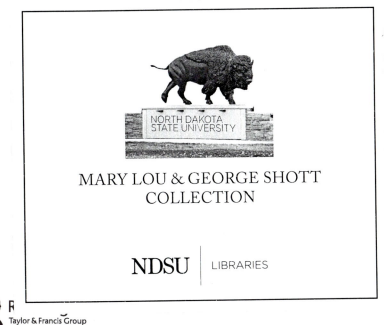

NORTH DAKOTA
STATE UNIVERSITY

MARY LOU & GEORGE SHOTT
COLLECTION

NDSU | LIBRARIES

R
Taylor & Francis Group
NEW YORK AND LONDON

First published 2020
by Routledge
52 Vanderbilt Avenue, New York, NY 10017

and by Routledge
2 Park Square, Milton Park, Abingdon, Oxon, OX14 4RN

Routledge is an imprint of the Taylor & Francis Group, an informa business

Library of Congress Cataloging-in-Publication Data
Names: RePass, David E., author.
Title: Listening to the American voter: what was on voters' minds
in presidential elections, 1960 to 2016/David E. RePass.
Description: New York, NY: Routledge, 2020. | Includes
bibliographical references and index.
Identifiers: LCCN 2019056477 (print) | LCCN 2019056478 (ebook) |
ISBN 9780367467470 (hardback) | ISBN 9780367819675 (paperback) |
ISBN 9781003030829 (ebook)
Subjects: LCSH: Presidents—United States—Election—History—
20th century. | Presidents—Untied States—Election—History—
21st century. | Voting research—United States. | United States—Politics
and government—Public opinion.
Classification: LCC JK524 .R457 2020 (print) | LCC JK524 (ebook) |
DDC 324.973/092—dc23
LC record available at https://lccn.loc.gov/2019056477
LC ebook record available at https://lccn.loc.gov/2019056478

ISBN: 978-0-367-46747-0 (hbk)
ISBN: 978-0-367-81967-5 (pbk)
ISBN: 978-1-003-03082-9 (ebk)

Typeset in Bembo
by codeMantra

To the American voter

CONTENTS

FIGURES

TABLES

PREFACE

This book presents a method of accurately measuring the mandate in presidential elections. It finds what voters liked and disliked about the candidates, the problems voters were concerned with and wanted solved, and the role of party identification. After finding what voters were thinking about these factors, my method measures the exact importance of each factor in the overall outcome of the election. The resulting finding is within ±1 percent of the actual outcome.

In a democracy, this information is invaluable. Our government is supposed to be guided by the will of the people. Thus, a correct reading of the mandate is vital. The book will show that, up to now, attempts to interpret the mandate have been based on unreliable data and faulty methods. For the first time, a method has been found to get a correct reading of the mandate.

In addition, the book will present a new way to measure the ideological composition of the American electorate. I will also deal with the question of the polarization of Congress; is it a reflection of a polarized public?

This book is the result of over thirty years of teaching electoral behavior and quantitative methods. The book explains the results of most presidential elections since 1960. All variables (except party identification and ideology) were measured with open-ended questions. These questions reveal the attitudes voters had in mind when making their decisions.

The book has one major reference: high-quality survey data from the American National Election Studies (ANES). These data provide *primary source* information on the thoughts of the voters. With two exceptions (Converse, 1966 and Stokes, 1958), secondary analyses found in books and articles by political scientists were not used. Except where noted, all data in the book were from the ANES and all tables were statistically significant at the .001 level.

My measures and methods are original, repeatedly replicated, and carefully tested for validity. The methods are totally unique, so naturally my results will differ from most other studies based on other methods. Appendices will be used to explain the details of my methods and measures along with a comparison of them with relevant past studies of voting behavior.

My methods cannot be used when there is a three-dimensional dependent variable; that is, when there is a third party candidate who wins a substantial number of votes as did Wallace in 1968 and Perot in 1992. Therefore, the 1968 and 1992 election will not be analyzed.

ACKNOWLEDGMENTS

This book would not have been possible if it were not for data from the American National Election Studies (ANES) and that data would not have been collected if not for the Principal Investigators. These men and women devoted an enormous amount of their time to overseeing these studies, yet they are seldom given the recognition they deserve. Their names are listed in the Reference section of the book.

I also want to acknowledge my friends and mentors Phil Converse and Don Stokes for their pioneering contributions to the analysis of the ANES surveys. Converse's conception and measurement of the "normal vote" informed one of my major theoretical constructs, and I used Stokes' component analysis to measure the exact causes of election outcomes.

Data for the 2016 election would not have been available if I did not have help coding the open-ended verbatim comments. Tim Snider, Grace Suttle, Jean Goeppinger, and Janet Morrow gave me that help.

And, finally, I want to thank my students over the years for being a critical sounding board for my ideas.

INTRODUCTION

In every election, there are two campaigns—the campaign as seen through the eyes of the political elite and the campaign as seen and evaluated by ordinary voters. The political elite consists of the candidates and their advisers, reporters and media commentators, political admen, pollsters, and other political analysts. In many respects, the campaign is a *dialog among these elites*. They discuss issues that *they* think are important, major newspapers provide topics for the day's discussion by news channel commentators, moderators of debates are well-known media commentators who choose which questions to ask, and the producers of TV news programs select which snippets of candidates' speeches to show. The media atmosphere is filled with paid ads and counter-ads. And so on. There is a cacophony of stimuli emanating from the political elite. The question is: how much of it is absorbed by voters and influences their decisions? Just because a great deal of attention is given to an issue or to an aspect of a candidate by the political elite does not mean that it was an important factor in voters' decisions. Furthermore, we must be aware that voters have their own priorities and perspectives. They look directly at the candidates and make their own evaluations, and they decide which events and conditions are important enough to be concerned about.

The only way we can know which of these elements have become part of the voter's decision process is to use open-ended questions to learn what they have paid attention to. *We need to see the campaign as voters see it.*

In this book, two basic open-ended questions will be used: a question that asks respondents what they like and dislike about the candidates and a question that asks what issues or problems they are concerned with, along with the party they think would be better to handle it. The answers, given in their own words, without prompts, give us a picture of what was on their minds.

It should be emphasized that in this book we are examining the factors proximate to the voting decision—what was in the forefront of voters' minds as they went into the voting booth? Background factors, such as ideology, may well influence issue concerns and attitudes toward candidates, but it is those concerns and attitudes that ultimately determine the voter's decision.

My Basic Model

As I began this book, I hypothesized that there were four variables that explain voting behavior: attitudes toward the Republican candidate, attitudes toward the Democratic candidate, party identification, and issues. If we know these four things about voters, I theorized, we can explain their vote. The following Model Equation was used to prove this contention. The Model Equation is based on Stokes (1958).

Note that we are working with bipolar dimensions (right and left) throughout this book. Mathematically, it is necessary to have a way to distinguish partisan direction and that is done with +'s and −'s. When Stokes performed his regression analysis in the 1950s, the Democrats were the ascendant party so he set up his equation so that a plus would represent the Democratic direction, and minus the Republican direction. I simply followed that precedent. Thus, if the Model Equation produces a negative result, that means the respondent will vote Republican.

Model Equation

$$\text{Vote} = \beta_1 DC - \beta_2 RC + \beta_3 PID + \beta_4 MIP$$

where DC = Attitude toward Democratic Candidate
RC = Attitude toward Republican Candidate
PID = Party Identification
MIP = Most Important Issue (problem)

The Model Equation is a standardized multiple regression which determines the importance (β) of each independent variable (the variables to the right of the equal sign) in explaining the dependent variable (vote). The βs are known as beta weights. In regression analysis, the weight of each independent variable is calculated while controlling or holding constant the other independent variables. This means that each beta weight is a measure of the importance of just that variable without being influenced by the other independent variables.

Attitudes toward candidates (DC and RC) were measured by the American National Election Studies (ANES) open-ended questions, which ask, "Is there anything in particular about [candidate X] that might make you want to vote for him?" "... against him?" Answers to this question are recorded verbatim by the interviewer. Following are some examples of typical kinds of things respondents said in answer to these questions. The few examples here cannot begin to represent the great variety of comments made and are far from being the full set of candidate attributes that were present in the example elections.[1] A full summary of all comments made in all elections will be found in the profiles of the candidates in Chapter 4. The verbatims here are presented to give the reader the "flavor" of what is contained in the attitude toward candidate variable.

From 1964 Election Study

LIKE ABOUT LBJ: I like his attitude toward the Negroes.
DISLIKE ABOUT LBJ: No.
LIKE ABOUT GOLDWATER: Nothing.
DISLIKE ABOUT GOLDWATER: His attitude toward the Civil Rights bill.

LIKE ABOUT LBJ: Well, he's well qualified. He's proven he can get support. He's had a lot of experience and has handled all issues well in the change-over from Kennedy. He's going to take his time on an issue and not "cock his gun" too fast and get us in war.
DISLIKE ABOUT LBJ: Nothing.
LIKE ABOUT GOLDWATER: I believe he's honest and would the best he knows how.
DISLIKE ABOUT GOLDWATER: His statements about foreign relations. He's too quick to make a snap decision and this might get us in trouble.

LIKE ABOUT LBJ: He has done a lot with the poverty bill. I'm glad he is following in Kennedy's footsteps.
DISLIKE ABOUT LBJ: No.
LIKE ABOUT GOLDWATER: No.
DISLIKE ABOUT GOLDWATER: He is hasty in decision. I don't trust him. He frightens me.

From 1968 Election Study

LIKE HUMPHREY: He come across to me as a very sincere person, genuine and honest. He is compassionate.
DISLIKE HUMPHREY: He talks too much.
LIKE NIXON: Only that he seems to be remarkably well-organized.

DISLIKE NIXON: I have a deep-seated feeling that he is not trustworthy. He does not come through to me as an honest and open person. He wants to advance himself to the point of being unprincipled.

LIKE WALLACE: Nothing.

DISLIKE WALLACE: He rules Alabama like Hitler ruled Germany. He promotes fear rather than respect. I consider him ignorant, unprincipled, and dangerous.

LIKE HUMPHREY: I agree with the progressive legislation that he has advanced since the late 1940s. I feel that he is sincere. I trust him and that is important in a candidate.

DISLIKE HUMPHREY: The unfortunate tie he has with decisions made by President Johnson—the handling of the Vietnam War.

LIKE NIXON: Well, I like the party alright. I think they have a better stand on crime and violence. I believe he is in a better position to negotiate terms on the Vietnam War.

DISLIKE NIXON: I think he may be prone to act without sufficient thought and study. I don't think he is a dynamic leader.

LIKE WALLACE: Nothing!

DISLIKE WALLACE: Wallace stands for everything I'm against, particularly white supremacy.

LIKE HUMPHREY: Nothing.

DISLIKE HUMPHREY: He hasn't done anything to solve the Vietnam War.

LIKE NIXON: I think he may try to stop the war and stop these stupid race riots.

DISLIKE NIXON: Nothing.

LIKE WALLACE: He definitely wants to stop all this rioting. He will bring the country back to where it should be. He will bring in the police and enforce law. After listening to him on TV, I think he means what he says.

From 2008 Election Study

LIKE OBAMA: His sincerity. He cares about people regardless of color. He wants to make change.

DISLIKE OBAMA: Nothing.

LIKE MCCAIN: Nothing.

DISLIKE MCCAIN: Can't depend on him to help low income people. He's too old.

LIKE OBAMA: Intelligence, common sense, and youth. Enthusiasm.

DISLIKE OBAMA: Nothing.

LIKE MCCAIN: Older and more experienced

DISLIKE MCCAIN: Views on continuing the war, offshore drilling

LIKE OBAMA: Truly inspiring, never had a leader that will inspire us like him. Very credible and you believe him.

DISLIKE OBAMA: Nothing.

LIKE MCCAIN: Service record, protected his fellow soldiers. Before he started campaigning, he was more moderate on energy independence and changed on conservation.

DISLIKE MCCAIN: He is too old and his choice of VP (Palin) could be the next president and that is not good.

From 2016 Election Study

LIKE CLINTON: Life spent in public service, a great deal of political experience, knowledge of foreign affairs, emphasis on children and families.

DISLIKE CLINTON: Nothing.

LIKE TRUMP: Nothing.

DISLIKE TRUMP: Elitist, racist, invokes hate, he's not educated in politics, untrustworthy, rude.

LIKE CLINTON: Her experience. Her husband having served as president for eight years, there's nobody better to have on your bench then someone that has had the job. She makes calculated decisions and doesn't shoot from the hip.

DISLIKE CLINTON: Nothing.

LIKE TRUMP: Nothing.

DISLIKE TRUMP: I think he is most obnoxious and is racist for sure. His temper is out of control. He makes me nervous. He doesn't listen to even his own people in his campaign. He's gonna do what he wants no matter what. We need someone who will talk to foreign leaders and doesn't have his mind made up already.

LIKE CLINTON: She's not Donald Trump.

DISLIKE CLINTON: Nothing.

LIKE TRUMP: Nothing.

DISLIKE TRUMP: His presentation; yikes, so much. His anger level is frightening.

LIKE CLINTON: No!

DISLIKE CLINTON: After President Clinton went through all the issues with impeachment and affairs, she stayed with him for her own political gain and power. Her judgment is awful. When you have an ambassador hundreds of times requesting more security and she doesn't get the job done. (reference to Benghazi). Untrustworthy with the emails and all of that.

LIKE TRUMP: I am aligned with him on all his positions. Closing the border and building a wall, lower taxes, helping the vets, strong military, and especially fair trade and stopping outsourcing. He is not a typical politician and has a proven track record in business success. He's straight forward.

DISLIKE TRUMP: Nothing.

The party identification variable (PID) was measured by the question, "Generally speaking, do you usually think of yourself as a Republican, a Democrat, an Independent, or what?" Those who answer "Republican" or "Democrat" are then asked, "Would you call yourself a strong [Democrat/Republican] or not very strong [Democrat/Republican]?" Those who answer "not very strong" are usually referred to as "weak Republican" or "weak Democrat."[2]

The issue question (MIP) is, "What do you think are the most important problems facing the country?" Up to three issues are recorded. Respondents are then asked, "Which political party do you think would be the most likely to get the government to do a better job in dealing with the problem mentioned?" It is the answer to this question that gives the issue a partisan valence.[3]

Table 0.1 shows the results of applying the regression analysis to most elections since 1960. To understand the Model Equation results, let us look, for example, at the 1960 regression equation in Table 0.1. This equation can be read as follows: the .25 beta weight for JFK means that for each degree of increase in attitude toward JFK, the respondent was 25 percent more likely to vote for him. The attitude toward Nixon weight of − .33 means that for each degree of increase in attitude toward Nixon, there was a 33 percent increase in the likelihood of a Republican vote. (Remember, minus means Republican direction.)

PID was measured on a scale ranging from Strong Democrat (scale position ("+2")), through Weak Democrat ("+1"), Independent ("0"), Weak Republican ("−1"), to Strong Republican ("−2"). The .24 beta weight for this variable in 1960 meant that for each degree of increase in strength of Democratic identification, there was a 24 percent increase in likelihood of voting for Kennedy.

Finally, the MIP variable was measured by the question that ascertained which party the respondent thought would be best to handle the problem the respondent felt was most important. Its weight was .17. That means that those respondents who thought one of the parties would be best to handle the issue were 17 percent more likely to vote for that party.

TABLE 0.1 Application of the Model Equation 1960–2016

	Percent of Cases Correctly Estimated	Degree of Correlation (R)
1960 Vote = .25JFK − .33Nixon + .24PID + .17MIP	95%	.84
1964 Vote = .29LBJ − .34AuH$_2$O + .21PID + .18MIP	96%	.85
1976 Vote = .26Carter − .29Ford + .23PID + .25MIP	94%	.82
1980 Vote = .35Carter − .20Reagan + .25PID + .22MIP	95%	.83
1984 Vote = .27Mondale − .38Reagan + .16PID + .18MIP	96%	.85
1988 Vote = .30Dukakis − .26HWBush + .25PID + .20MIP	96%	.85
1996 Vote = .43Clinton − .22Dole + .25PID + .11MIP	97%	.88
2000 Vote = .24Gore − .31WBush + .24PID + .21MIP	96%	.85
2004 Vote = .27Kerry − .42WBush + .15PID + .17MIP	97%	.89
2016 Vote = .35HClinton − .37Trump + .24 PID + .06MIP	96%	.85

The ANES studies from the years 1968, 1972, 1992, 2008, and 2012 did not contain the measures necessary to compute the Model Equation. The 1968 and 1992 NES studies did not offer respondents the opportunity to answer "Wallace" (in 1968) or "Perot" (in 1992) when asked, "Which party do you think will do a better job in dealing with the problem?" These third-party candidates were running on issues and received a significant share of the vote (14 and 19 percent respectively), yet their third parties were not included in the MIP measure. Also, the Model Equation cannot be used with a three-dimensional dependent variable. In the 1972 study, there were two separate samples, and, unfortunately, the candidate questions were in one sample and the problems question was in the other. Open-ended data in the 2008 and 2012 studies had not yet been coded when this book was written.

The Model Equation did a remarkably good job in explaining the vote. To verify this ability, data for each respondent was introduced into the equation, one respondent at a time. The respondent's score on each of the independent variables was weighted by the beta weight of that variable and these weighted scores then added up to find the predicted vote. The vote predicted or estimated by the equation *matched the actual vote over 95 percent of the time.* There are ten Model Equations shown in Table 0.1, ten replications, each worked well to explain vote year after year. The reliability of this method is clear. (A detailed explanation and methodological discussion of the Model Equation is presented in Appendix A.)

However, we should be aware that not every individual weighed each independent variable exactly the same. Some may have decided almost solely based on their party identification. Others may have been mostly influenced by their attitudes toward a particular candidate. And so forth. The beta weights in these equations average out these differences and give an aggregate, overall degree of influence of each of the independent variables.[4]

In looking over the data in Table 0.1, we see that, in each election, the candidates were by far the most heavily weighted factor. Each candidate *alone* was a very important factor in most elections; both candidates taken together accounted for, on average, 60 percent of the vote choice. Nonetheless, party identification and most important issue (MIP) each weighed a considerable amount, an average of 20 percent each. (There is one exception, in 2016 the MIP variable contributed almost nothing and the candidates contributed 72 percent. The 2016 election was very unusual—an aberration—with Donald Trump a major force. As we will see later, Trump himself was a most important problem in the eyes of many voters.)

Other Variables Often Used to Explain Vote

At this point, the reader may wonder why variables traditionally used to explain vote, such as ideology, issue questions from polls, and demographics, were not included in the Model Equation. The answer is, they were tried and did not add anything to the equation's ability to explain voting behavior. Beta weights for these variables were negligible.

Many pre-formulated, fixed-choice issue questions—the kind that are used in commercial opinion polls and exit polls—were asked in the ANES surveys. I tested each of these fixed-choice questions from ANES surveys by substituting them for the MIP variable the Model Equation. I took every such closed-ended issue question in every ANES survey over the last twenty-five years—all 266 of them—and entered them into the Model Equation, one at a time, to see if they produced a significant beta weight. I performed 266 regression analyses. Only nine of these fixed-choice issues produced a significant beta weight. (A weight of .06 was all that was required to be significant, a value much less than the MIP weights in Table 0.1.) The reasons why closed-ended issue questions do not help explain vote will be discussed at length in Chapter 3.

Adding a measure of ideology to the equation produced no significant beta weight. The fact that ideology is not directly related to vote is contrary to almost all polls which consistently show this relationship. Several reasons why my finding is true will be explained in Chapter 6, but for now let us look at one of the reasons—the correlation of ideology with vote is spurious. *Spuriousness* occurs when a third variable is causing the relationship—a third variable that is highly related to the two variables being correlated. In this case, that third variable is party identification. Party identification is highly related to vote and also to ideology. When this third variable is controlled, that is, held constant, the original correlation between ideology and vote becomes much smaller or disappears. (This will be explained in Appendix A.) In multiple regression equations, each independent variable is held constant while the effects of the other independent variables are measured. Party identification is one of the independent variables in the Model Equation and is held constant when ideology is one of the other independent variables in the equation. With party identification held constant, there is no significant correlation between ideology and vote. Most pollsters report only bivariate correlations and do not run controls. Without controlling for party identification, there appears to be a correlation between ideology and vote.

The role of demographics will be discussed in Chapter 2.

We can conclude that the Model Equation shows that the four variables I hypothesized would explain vote do indeed explain vote.

Notes

1 The only verbatim data available to me was from the 1964, 1968, 2008, and 2016 elections. The ANES is very concerned about protecting the anonymity of respondents. Open-ended comments could reveal who the respondent was and thus special permission is needed from the ANES to see this open-ended material.

2 Many surveys, including ANES surveys, ask an additional question of those who respond "Independent:" "Do you think of yourself as closer to the Republican Party or to the Democratic Party?" After extensive research, I have found that the answer to this "closer" question usually reflects respondents' current voting intention, not their long-term identity. It is important that the measure of PID be long-term identity. Furthermore, the "closer" question is a "push poll" where respondents are pushed into partisanship when basically they are non-partisan.

3 In early ANES studies, this "better job dealing" question was asked after each issue mentioned. In later studies, it was asked only with regard to the one issue respondents felt was most important. This is unfortunate since the full effect of all issue concerns was not measured and thus the weight of issues in the Model Equation is less that it should be.

4 The assumption that averaging is taking place is borne out by the high amount of variation explained (R^2) by the total equation. If a lot of respondents based their choice on just one or two factors (i.e., PID or a particular candidate), there would be a lot of variation that could not be explained.

Reference

Stokes, Donald E. 1958. "Components of Electoral Decision." *The American Political Science Review*, 52 (June): 367–387.

1

LONG-TERM FORCES

There are three important long-term factors in any election. Party identification is the major one. It is among the considerations proximate to the point of decision but also influences the formation of attitudes toward the candidates and issues. The other two long-term factors are involvement and ideology. Involvement is important since it determines whether someone will even bother to vote and contribute to the collective decision process. Ideology will be discussed in Chapter 6.

Involvement

The degree of individual involvement is strongly affected by five factors: personal interest in the election, strength of party identification, strength of ideological beliefs, sense of citizen duty, and roots in the community.[1] There is an important additional factor: stimulation—the overall excitement, media attention, and importance of the election. The stimulation effect can be seen when we look at turnout in presidential election years compared with off-year congressional elections. An average of 58 percent of the potential electorate[2] turns out in presidential years; 41 percent in off-year elections. Presidential elections are given overwhelming attention by the media, are exciting, and the choice of who is to be president is considered very important.

In a presidential year, if a voter possesses any one of the attributes that influence turnout—whether it be interest in politics or strong party identity or strong belief system or sense of duty or roots in the community—about 85 percent will cast a ballot. If two or more of these qualities are present, up to a 95 percent participation can be expected. If none of these qualities is present, turnout goes down to 40 percent or less.

A well-known observation about turnout is that young people are not likely to vote. The reasons older people do turnout helps to explain this. Young people are not likely to have established roots in a community and are in the process of developing their political beliefs and identity.

One would think that if someone does not feel that their vote counts (that they are only one among millions), or think the outcome of the election is already certain, he or she would be less inclined to vote. This is not the case. It may not seem "rational" to vote even if you know the other side will win or your vote will not count, but citizens rise above this calculating (cost–benefit) way of thinking. The effort to vote is motivated by internal, personal attitudes such as strong like for a candidate, ideology, party identification, interest, or sense of duty. Voters are self-motivated and will vote regardless of things like possibility of winning or the weather. An example of this was shown in an interesting study by Lang and Lang (1968). Years ago, votes were counted in the East and the results broadcast before many of those on the West Coast had voted. Lang and Lang conducted a survey in which they identified potential Goldwater voters in California who had not voted. These voters were divided into two groups—those who had seen broadcasts from the East, which showed that Goldwater would lose badly, and those who had not seen these broadcasts. Those who had seen the broadcasts voted anyway.

There is an external factor that may spur motivation to vote for those who lack the attributes discussed above. That is personal contact from a campaign worker who has made the effort to come to someone's home. Green and Gerber (2015) show that this works.

Party Identification

Now, let us look at party identification. When you identify with something, you feel part of it. Recall that the ANES question asks, "generally speaking, do you think of yourself as a Republican/Democrat?" The question that Gallup and many other commercial pollsters use is "In politics, *as of today*, do you consider yourself a Republican, Democrat, or Independent?" This does not measure long-term identity but rather current voting intention of the respondent. Note the difference between the Gallup wording ("as of today") and the ANES wording ("generally speaking, do you think of yourself as ...").

Those with a strong identity feel that they are part of the party. They feel good when their party wins and sad if it loses. They follow news of the party in newspapers, in magazines, on TV, and the Internet. They know the principal leaders. And, of course, they turn out and almost always vote for their party in every election. Then there are those with a less strong attachment to a party, the Weak Identifiers. They are less involved with party but nonetheless think of themselves as a Republican or a Democrat. They usually vote for its candidates but can fairly easily be persuaded to vote for the other side on occasion.

And finally, there are the Independents who are not attached to either party and therefore see politics in a non-partisan way.

Party identification is developed early in life and solidifies, usually by the time one is thirty. Parents are a major influence in acquiring a party identification; many children know by the time they are ten years old whether they are little Republicans or little Democrats. Another influence is social environment (neighborhood and friends). Also, a particularly appealing president (i.e., FDR, JFK, Reagan) can impress new voters and make them lifelong identifiers.

Realignment

Realignment is a change in the overall distribution of party identifiers in a state or in the nation such that one party adds a significant number (3 percent or more) to its ranks. There can also be dealignment in which there is a shift toward being Independent. These changes take place due to population replacement, that is, a disproportionate number of young, new voters coming into the electorate identifying with a certain party or, at the state level, a disproportionate number of a certain party migrating into the state. Realignment can also take place due to the conversion of people from one party to another.

Figure 1.1 shows the distribution of party identifiers and Independents over the period under study in this book.[3]

Looking at Figure 1.1, we see that there was a dip or trough in Republican identifiers from 1964 to around 1980. This was due to a realignment among African-Americans. For many decades before 1964, about 15 percent

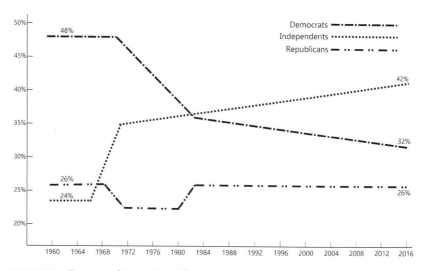

FIGURE 1.1 Percent of Party Identifiers and Independents, 1960–2016.

of African-Americans identified with the Republican Party. It was, after all, the party of Abraham Lincoln. Then in 1964, the Republican candidate, Barry Goldwater, sent a very clear signal to African-Americans that the Republican Party was not the party for them. In the midst of the 1964 election campaign, Goldwater, who was a Senator, voted against a Civil Rights bill. This vote was highly visible. By 1968, only 3 percent of African-Americans were still Republicans. This loss of a chunk of identifiers caused the dip we see in Figure 1.1. This is an example of realignment by conversion.

The second major change we see in Figure 1.1 is from around 1964 to 1984. This was due to realignment in the South. In the century following the Civil War, Southerners abhorred Republicans; they had subjected the South to the Radical Reconstruction and "damn Yankee" Republican carpetbaggers came South to plunder and take advantage of votes from the newly freed blacks to gain political office. For many decades after the Civil War, no white Southerner would think of being a Republican. Then, in the mid-1960s, the Democratic Congress and the Democratic president (LBJ) passed three laws that were anathema to the South: The Civil Rights Act, the Voting Rights Act, and discrimination in public accommodations was outlawed. Southerners left the Democratic Party in droves between 1964 and 2000; two-thirds of them became Independents and a third were now willing to call themselves Republicans. These additional Republicans filled the trough of departing African-Americans that had begun in 1964. Many politicians in the South switched labels from Democrat to Republican. Southerners have always been conservative, and this realignment brought consonance between this conservative ideology and party identity.

The Southern realignment was complete by 2000, yet the steady decline in Democrats continued nationally. By 2016, only 32 percent of the electorate identified with the Democratic Party. At the same time, as we will see in Chapter 6, the proportion of those with liberal belief systems increased. In particular, the proportion of strong liberals increased from 8 percent in 1992 to 20 percent in 2016. How did this inverse relationship come about—Democratic Party identification trending in one direction and liberal belief systems trending in the opposite direction? An examination of the data will reveal why this has happened.

We need to start in the 1930s when identity with the Democratic Party was at its zenith. FDR and the New Deal were very popular. Under the New Deal, government programs such as Social Security, making jobs available through the Works Project Administration (WPA) and the Civilian Conservation Corps (CCC), regulation of banks (Glass–Steagall), empowering unions, and so forth, lifted the ordinary American worker out of the depression. The New Deal had initiated programs that greatly expanded the role of government in helping ordinary people and regulating the economy. New, young voters were especially attracted to the Democratic Party in the 1930s. They were the primary reason the party had swelled its ranks of identifiers to almost half the electorate.

By 1990, this surge of (now much older) Democratic identifiers were dying off but they were not being replaced by young, new Democrats. This was not for lack of young, new liberals. It is well known that each generation is more liberal than the last and thus the population is continually infused with those who believe in an active government, equality, are tolerant of those who are different, and generally accept change. This generational input of new, liberal voters over several decades is one of the reasons why blacks have gained their rights, why gays have become accepted, gay marriage permitted, and other liberal policies have been advanced.

An example of this generational infusion of liberals is the evolution of attitudes toward women's rights.

In Table 1.1 we see that each new cohort of young people contained more and more of those who gave the liberal answer (women should have equal rights). Half (51 percent) of the young cohort that started voting around 1976 were for equal rights for women while this was true of only 32 percent of older voters at that time. By 1998, young, new voters came into the electorate already very liberal about women's rights—82 percent favored them. One would expect that these new liberals would become Democrats and thus increase the ranks of Democrats. The opposite happened. As Table 1.1 shows, the proportion of new voters who entered the electorate as Democrats from 1976 to 1998 did not increase and then it started declining in 2000.

The reason that liberals were no longer joining the Democratic Party at the same rate as earlier is because Democratic leaders had taken down the liberal banner that FDR had put up with the New Deal—the banner that had attracted half of the electorate. *Without the banner, these new liberals saw no party to belong to.* Many became Independents. The banner went down because Democratic Party leaders mistakenly thought that McGovern's big loss in 1972 and Dukakis' loss in 1988 were due to the fact that they were liberals.[4] Party leaders decided never to use the word "liberal" and to steer clear of policies that

TABLE 1.1 Generational Change in Attitudes toward Women's Rights and Democratic Party Identification

	1976	1988	1998	2008	2016
Proportion of the Young* who favor equal rights for women	51%	73%	82%		
Proportion of the Young who are Democrats	34%	34%	34%	28%	24%

* Young = 18–30.

Based on the question: "Recently, there has been a lot of talk about women's rights. Some people feel that women should have an equal role with men in running businesses, industry, and the government. Others feel that women's place is in the home."

could allow them to be accused of being liberal. The older generation of New Deal Democrats were dying off and they were not being replaced. That is a sure formula for declining membership.

To summarize, the major finding of Figure 1.1 is that by 2016 there was a near balance between Democratic and Republican identifiers, with neither having anything close to a majority. Now Independents have become the dominant group.

Notes

1 Roots in the community is measured by home ownership.
2 The "potential electorate" are all those eligible to vote.
3 Rather than show jagged lines connecting each data point, averages were computed when data points were similar over a period of time. This method of presentation makes the graph easier to read and smooths out variation caused by sampling.
4 We will see in Chapter 4 that this was not the case, McGovern and Dukakis lost for non-ideological reasons.

References

Green, Donald, and Alan Gerber. 2015. *Get Out the Vote*, 3rd edition. Washington, DC: The Brookings Institution Press.
Lang, Kurt, and Gladys Engel Lang. 1968. *Voting and Nonvoting: Implications of Broadcasting Returns before Polls are Closed*. Waltham: Blaisdell Publishing.

2

SHORT-TERM FORCES

Each election cycle presents voters with new candidates and new issues. Even presidents running for a second term are not seen the same as when first elected. Voters can now judge their actual performance in office, see what problems they have created and what problems they have solved, etc. It is these short-term forces—candidates and issues—that produce change from one election to the next.

To find the effect of short-term forces, we need a stable point of reference from which to measure. Such a point is the hypothetical vote that would occur *if there were no short-term forces*—a "steady state" of the electorate. It would be the vote if party identification were the only factor.

The problem in finding this steady state was that no actual election had ever occurred that was devoid of at least some short-term forces. There has been no election based only on party identification that could serve as a model. Philip Converse (1966) found a way to measure this steady state, calling it the "normal vote."

The normal vote is based on the proportion of Strong Democrats, Weak Democrats, Independents, Weak Republicans, and Strong Republicans in the population. We saw in Chapter 1 that there was a high percentage of Democrats in the electorate in 1960; the normal vote at that time was 54 percent. By 2016, the proportion of Democrats had decreased considerably and the proportion of Independents had increased considerably; the normal vote was therefore close to 50–50.

Figures 2.1a, 2.1b, and 2.1c present a picture of how short-term forces affected each election, how many voters were swayed away from their party identity by short-term forces, and how much movement was there away from the normal vote. If the forces were strong and mostly in one partisan direction, the deflection is large; if the forces are slight or divided in the partisan direction, there was little change. A major point is that this deflection is only temporary—a result of the particular short-term forces that were unique to that election. As soon as the election is over, these deflectors "spring back" to their normal political positioning. (I use the term "deflection" rather than "defection" since "defection" would imply a permanent departure.)

The Converse method of calculating the normal vote is validated by looking at off-year congressional elections, which are based mainly on party identification as is the normal vote. In congressional elections, most voters do not know much about the candidates and there are usually no major issues. The short-term forces of candidate and issues are missing. We see in Figure 2.1 that in almost all off-year congressional elections, the total vote for congressmen across

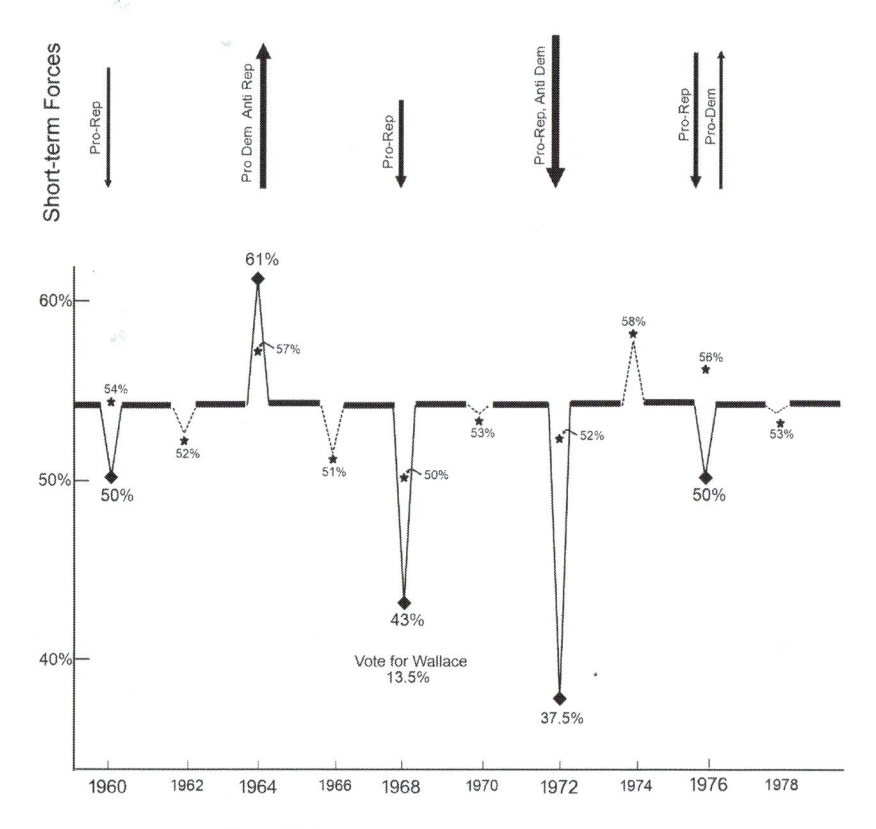

FIGURE 2.1a Deviation from Normal Democratic Vote, 1960–1978.

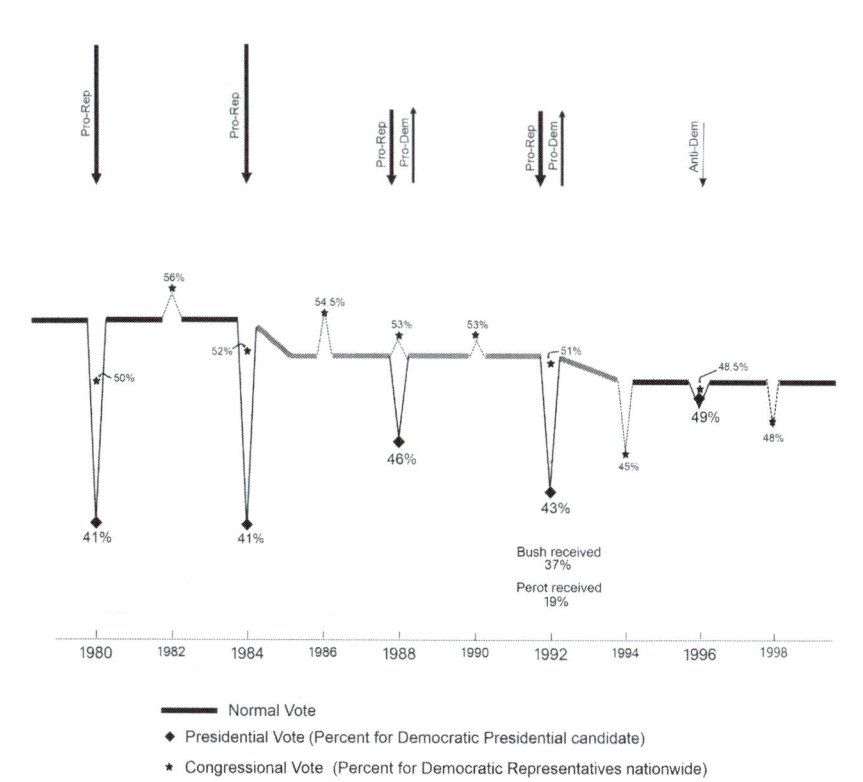

FIGURE 2.1b Deviation from Normal Democratic Vote, 1980–1998.

the country was within 3 percent of the normal vote. (This small amount of a variation is less than the sampling error.)

There were, however, six off-year elections, which deviated significantly from normal—1974, 1994, 2002, 2010, 2014, and 2018. The reasons for this were:

> The 1974 election was unusually pro-Democratic (anti-Nixon). This was the first election after the Watergate scandal, with its prolonged congressional investigation, and the ultimate near-impeachment of Nixon. The 1994 election, which Democrats lost badly, was orchestrated by a skilled strategist, Newt Gingrich. Also, one of the most important issues in 1994 was health care insurance which Clinton had promised to pass during the 1992 campaign. He could not get it done and that was a disappointment to many voters. The 2002 election came in the wake of 9/11, and the country gave support to their president. The 2010 election saw a major negative reaction to the Affordable Care Act. The unusual deflection toward Republicans

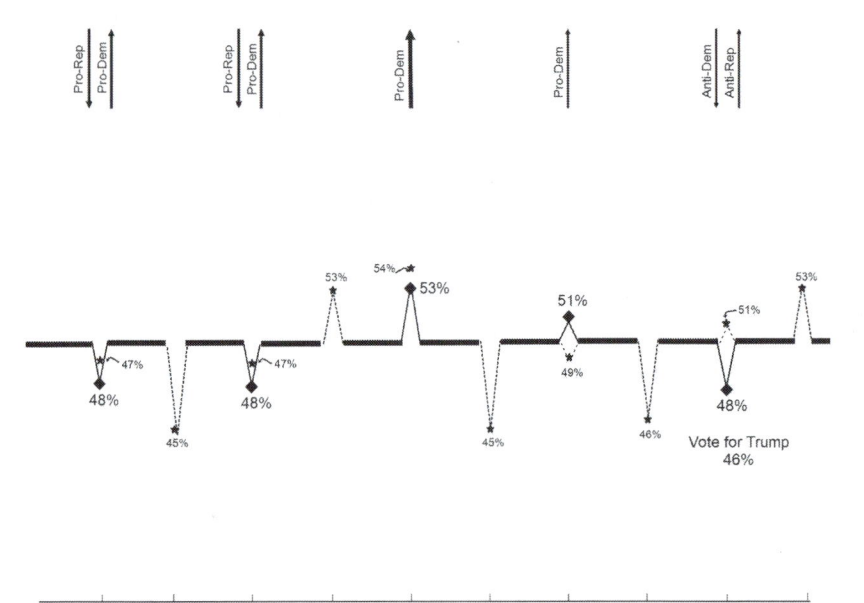

FIGURE 2.1c Deviation from Normal Democratic Vote, 2000–2018.

in 2014 is difficult to explain. It could be the result of precise, computerized, gerrymandering by the Republicans who had gained control of many state legislatures by the time of the 2010 census. It is the state legislatures that draw congressional districts and by 2014 many congressional districts had become non-competitive as a result of this gerrymandering. No Democratic candidate could be found to run in these non-competitive districts. With no Democrat to vote for, Democrats stayed home. The total vote for congressmen was thus devoid of many Democratic votes. The 2018 election was a reaction to the highly unpopular president Trump.

No Permanent Change or Trend

Note that Figure 2.1 is full of sharp peaks; there are no plateaus. No set of elections reaches a plateau where the nation has changed underlying political dispositions such as becoming more conservative, or more populist, more divisive, or isolationist, etc. Furthermore, even landslides, such as happened in 1964, 1972, 1980, 1984, and 1988, do not mark the permanent weakening of the party that was overwhelmed by the landslide. For example, Nixon, a Republican, was elected four years after Goldwater was crushed in 1964; Carter, the Democrat, was elected in 1976 after the McGovern debacle in 1972.

One of the biggest mistakes made by election analysts is to compare the results of the last election with the state of the electorate in the present election cycle. There is a tendency to compare the support a party's candidate received in the last election with polling data on the current campaign. Party strategists often think that if only they could count on or even build on the support their party had in the last election, they could win. The problem with this type of analysis is that it is measuring the distance between one moving point compared with another moving point. Even Einstein, the inventor of the theory of relativity, would have difficulty taking measurements in this situation. Another way to describe this phenomenon is to imagine trees that have been bent over by a high wind (i.e., short-term forces). If a snapshot were taken while the trees were in that position and, for the next two years, that picture was used to show what trees look like, the picture would be very misleading. In the real world, the trees would have "sprung back" to their normal positions.

We see in Figure 2.1 that in 1964, 1968, 1972, 1980, 1984, and 1992 there were major deflections in vote. In the rest of the elections, including all those since the millennium, deviation has been rather minor. As we have noted, attitudes toward candidates is the major factor in voter choice. Most of the major deflections came in elections where there was a very popular and/or a very unpopular candidate—1964: LBJ (very popular) vs. Goldwater (very unpopular); 1972: McGovern (very unpopular); 1980: Carter (very unpopular); 1984: Mondale (very unpopular). In 2016, both candidates were unpopular and the result was almost no net movement away from the normal vote.

Two general observations can be made from looking at Figure 2.1:

1   Political analysts often cite the fact that off-year congressional elections almost always result in a loss of seats by the party that won the presidency two years earlier. But why? The figure shows that in presidential elections, vote for Congress usually shifts in the direction of the winning presidential candidate. There is a coat-tail effect in presidential years. With this surge in congressional vote toward the winning candidate in presidential years, it is only natural that it would fall back to normal in off-years when the president is not on the ballot. In other words, the fallback in off-year congressional elections has little to do with the president's performance; it happens naturally as voters return to their normal vote.

2   Some political analysts and historians believe that there are periodic cycles in elections. Figure 2.1 shows over half a century of election results. There are no patterns or cycles. *Each election is sui generous.*

Deflection from Party Identification

Figures 2.3a, 2.3b, and 2.3c show graphically how much the short-term forces deflected voters away from their party identification. To picture this, I use an analogy of reeds in the wind, the wind being short-term forces. The explanatory Figure 2.2 shows five lines—reeds—each representing a type of party identification. There are strong (thick) reeds representing Strong Democrats and Strong Republicans, weak (thin) reeds representing Weak Democrats and Weak Republicans, and a vertical reed representing Independents. Strong reeds are hard to move and it takes a very strong wind to move them. The explanatory figure depicts the reeds in the absence of wind (short-term forces). In this "no-wind" situation, the party reeds are horizontal—on the ground showing no deflection. The Independent reed is vertical, indicating that it could go either way.

Now let us look at Figures 2.3a, 2.3b, and 2.3c. When the winds (short-term forces) are blowing predominately from left to right (in the Republican direction)—as they were in 1960, 1968, 1972, 1980, and 1984—the Democratic reeds are lifted up and blown in the Republican direction. Weak Democrats, in particular, are deflected as shown by the gray area under their reeds. When the winds are mainly blowing from right to left, as they were in 1964, the Weak Republican reed is lifted up considerably. (Throughout the figures, gray areas show the percent who were deflected.)

All the other elections had winds from both directions (cross-currents), thus rather small amounts of deflection among Weak Identifiers and Independents.

One of the most important things that can be seen in Figures 2.3a, 2.3b, and 2.3c is that Strong identifiers (Strong Republicans and Strong Democrats) are hardly affected at all by short-term forces; they remain loyal to their party. Even when there was a huge wind in the Democratic direction, as there was in 1964, 90 percent of Strong Republicans voted for Goldwater.

Another thing to note in the figures is, surprisingly, that Independents do not move as much as Weak Identifiers. It is the Weak Identifiers that can make or break a candidate. Under each party identification group is a

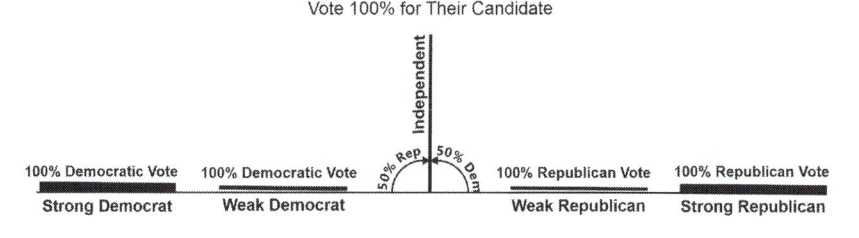

Reeds At Rest Assuming No Short-term Forces
Vote 100% for Their Candidate

FIGURE 2.2 Reeds Explanatory Figure.

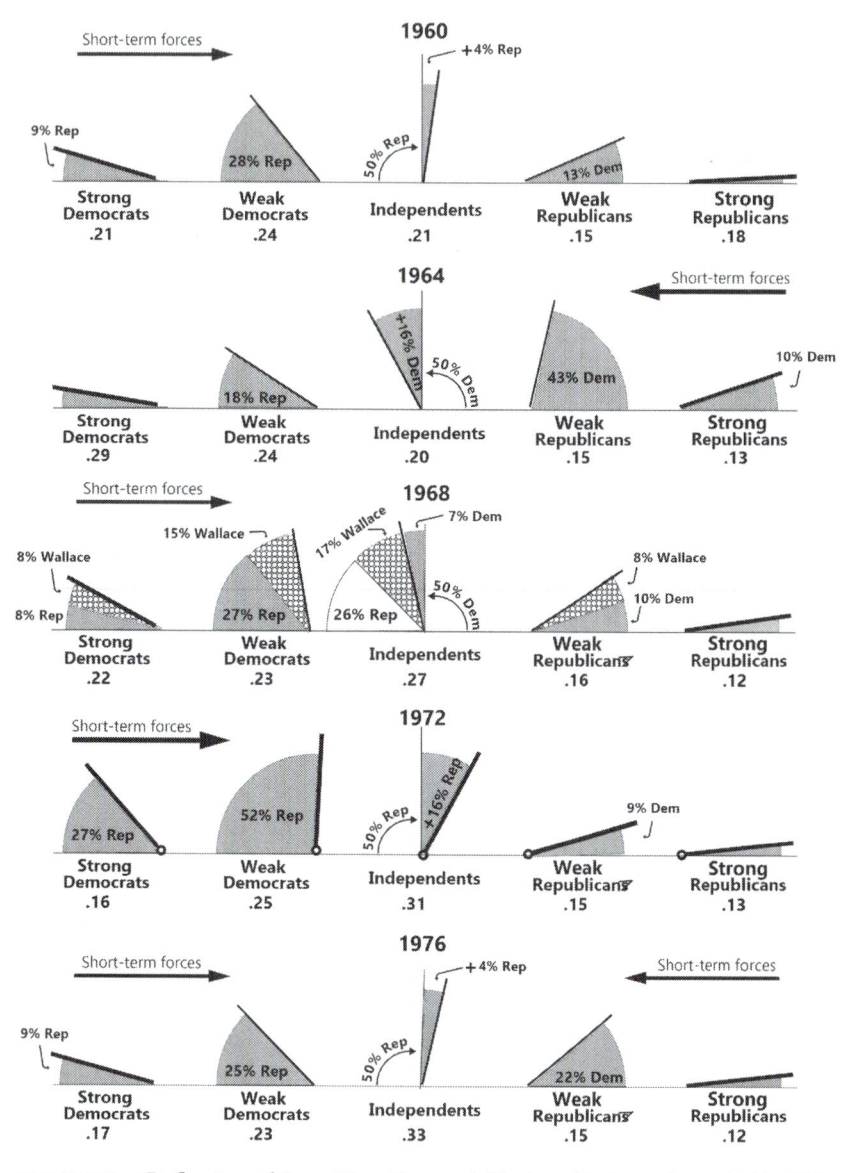

FIGURE 2.3a Deflection of Party Identifiers and Choice of Independents, 1960–1978.

decimal number that is the proportion of the total number of voters in the group. If the group had a high deflection rate, one can calculate how much of a party's potential vote was lost by deflection. In many elections, if only a candidate could have held on to more of his/her party identifiers, they would have won.

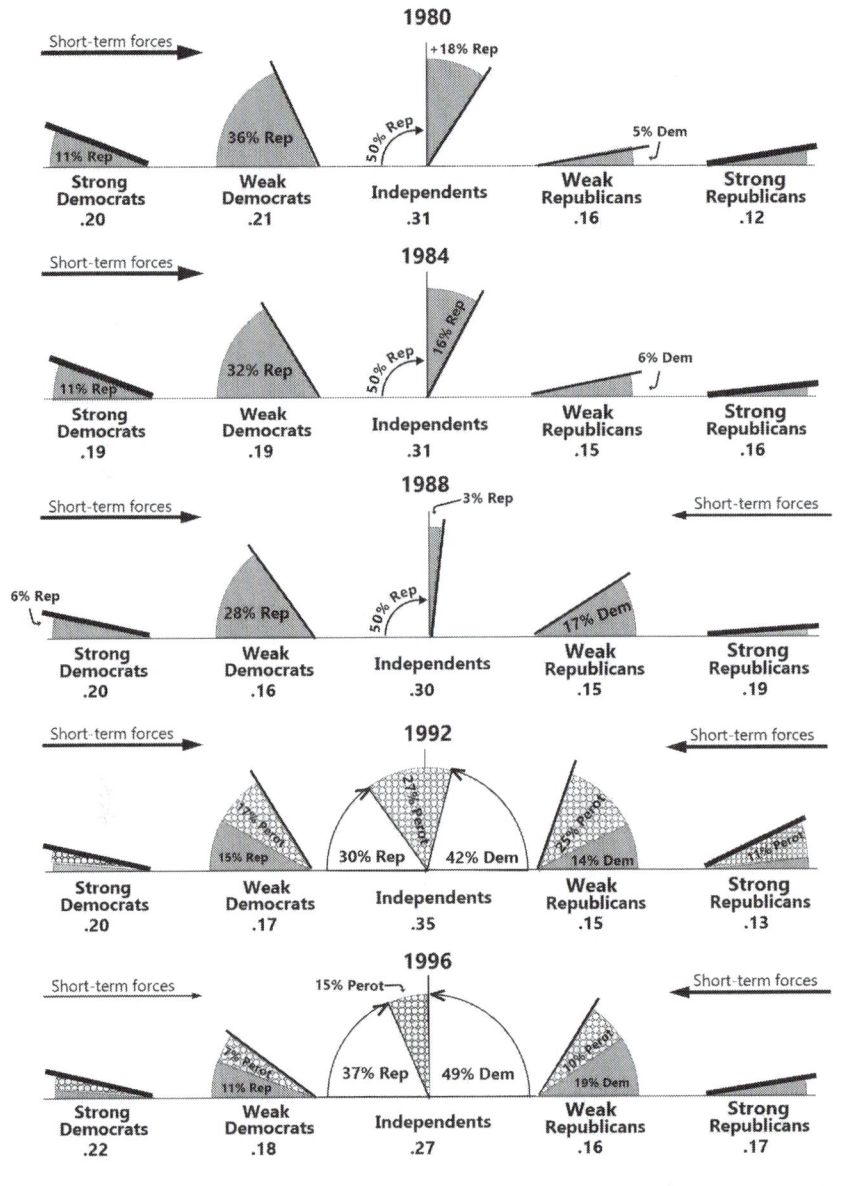

FIGURE 2.3b Deflection of Party Identifiers and Choice of Independents, 1980–1998.

In 1992, Ross Perot cost the Republicans more than the Democrats. Twenty-five percent of Weak Republicans voted for Perot compared with 17 percent of Weak Democrats. Note that the independent candidate (Perot) came in third among the Independents.

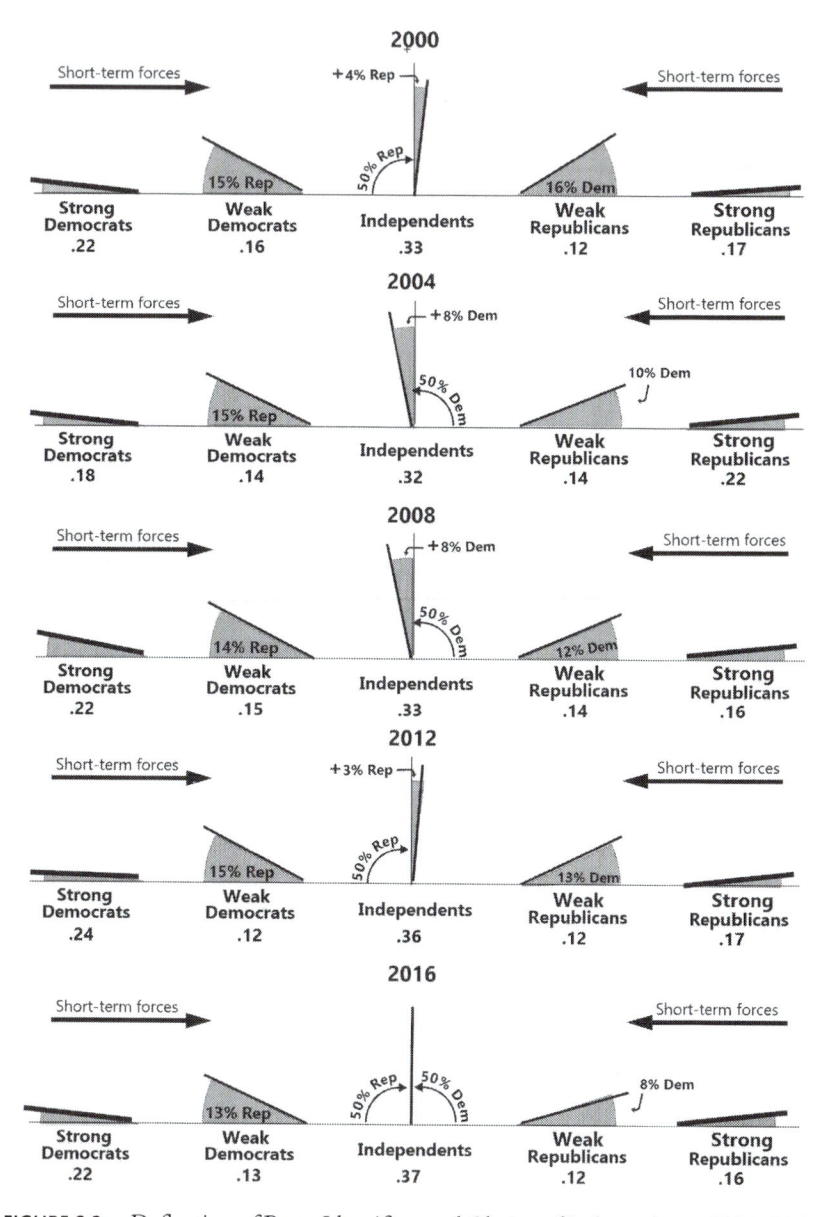

FIGURE 2.3c Deflection of Party Identifiers and Choice of Independents, 2000–2016.

The Role of Demographic Groups

In most analyses by pollsters, if they see that a certain demographic group is giving unusual support or unusual opposition to a candidate, they assume that it has something to do with the group they are in. In 2016, for example, analysts kept citing suburban women as an important factor in the election results. In other elections, it was "Joe the Plummer" (working-class) voters, and so forth. There are a number of reasons why demographics are a very poor way to explain voting behavior.

What Were Demographic Groups Thinking?

If a demographic group votes a certain way, we have no way of telling why. We do not know what they were thinking and what motivated them. Analysts assume they know just by the fact that the group supports a certain candidate. Whenever a group as a whole is characterized on the basis of assumed reasons for their behavior, that is stereotyping. You simply cannot know what people are thinking by looking at their gender or skin color, etc.

Categorization Is Not Group Identification

When processing their data, analysts place respondents into demographic categories. Respondents are not aware that they have been placed in a category (that they "belong" to this group), yet analysts think of them as "members" of that group. Respondents should be asked if they identify with the group if one is interested in identity politics.

All Demographic Groups Are Affected by the Same Short-term Forces

Short-term forces (candidates and issues) affect people from all walks of life. These forces are like the wind that is felt by everyone. *People from all demographic groups move in the same direction in an election.* In the following charts we will see how people from all demographic groups make similar evaluations of the candidates. If a candidate is seen positively, all groups move in the positive direction, and vice versa.

Also, most major issue concerns cut across all demographic groups as we will see in Chapter 3. For example, the issue of civil rights was a concern of a large number of voters in 1964—68 percent were white. Half of those concerned with racism in 2016 were white. Half of those concerned with education had no children. (This will be discussed further in Chapter 3.)

Figures 2.4a through 2.4f show the net attitudes of various demographic groups toward the presidential candidates in most elections since 1960. "Net attitudes" is measured by the number of positive remarks minus the negative remarks made by respondents to the open-ended questions, which ascertain likes and dislikes of the candidates.

The main thing to notice when looking at the demographic covariation figures is that attitudes toward candidates move *in tandem* across almost all demographic groups in all elections. This indicates that candidates are seen in a

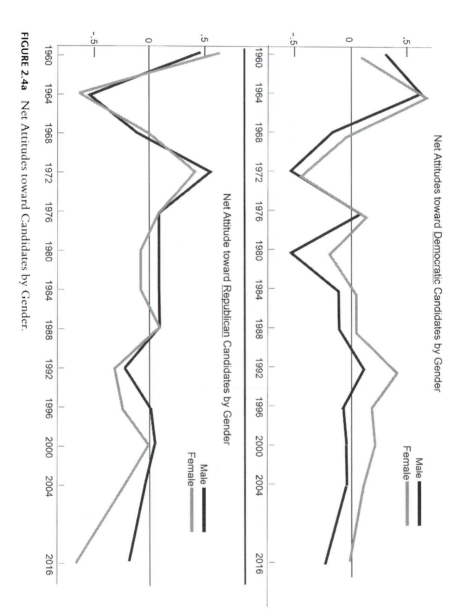

FIGURE 2.4a Net Attitudes toward Candidates by Gender.

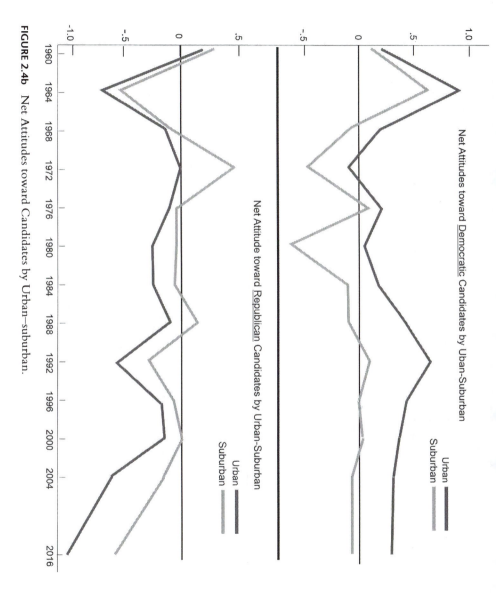

FIGURE 2.4b Net Attitudes toward Candidates by Urban–suburban.

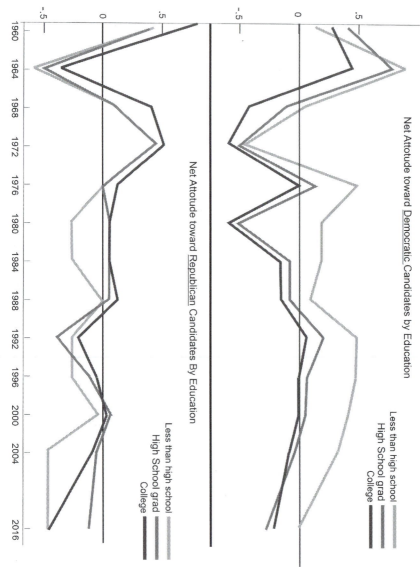

FIGURE 2.4c Net Attitudes toward Candidates by Education.

Net Attotude toward Democratic Candidates by Education

Net Attotude toward Republican Candidates By Education

Less than high school
High School grad
College

Less than high school
High School grad
College

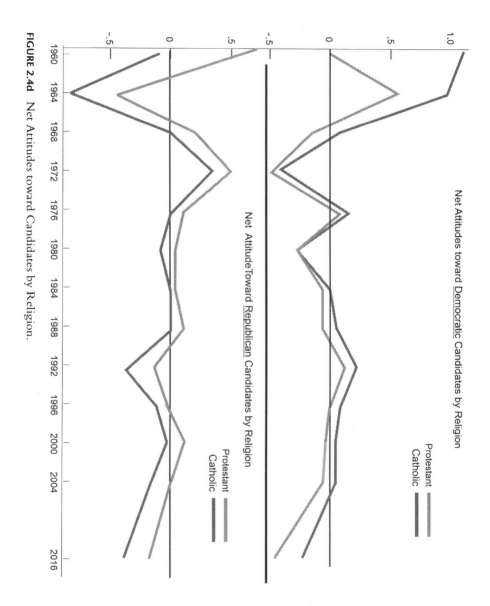

FIGURE 2.4d Net Attitudes toward Candidates by Religion.

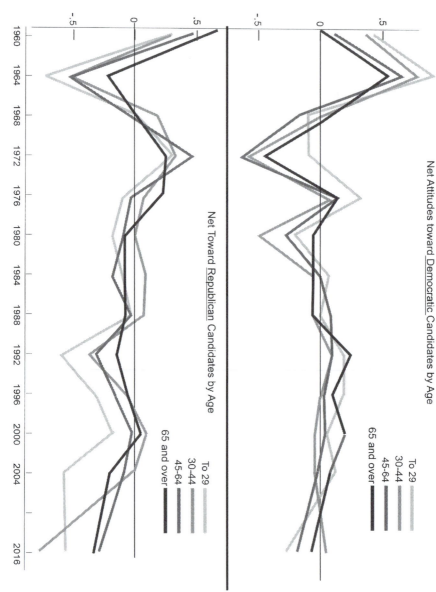

FIGURE 2.4e Net Attitudes toward Candidates by Age.

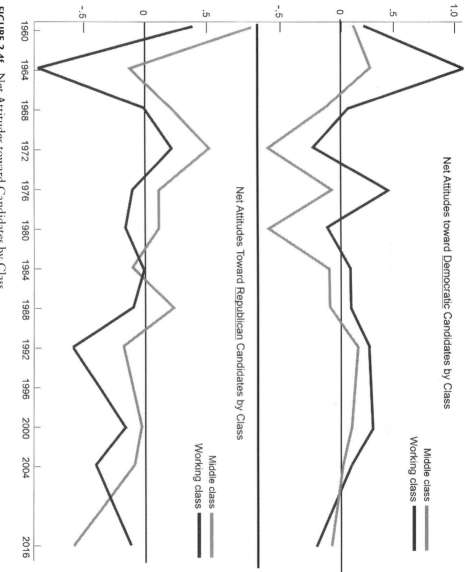

FIGURE 2.4f Net Attitudes toward Candidates by Class.

similar way regardless of the demographic group. In many cases, the lines of the graph are almost on top of each other.

In some of the covariation figures, there is some space between groups—the groups run parallel but with a gap in between. This is especially noticeable in the Urban–Suburban and Gender Figures. This gap is due to differences to party identification in these groups—urban dwellers tend to be Democrats and suburban, Republican. Women tend to be Democrats. When pollsters isolate these groups in their analyses, they are often really looking at party identification.

A graph of the attitudes of African-Americans is not shown since they change little from election to election and are far apart from whites at all times. They are almost all Democrats.

Of the 182 comparisons shown in these covariation figures, there were only three instances in which attitudes between groups did not move in tandem. Two of those instances involved a situation in which a group qua group could appropriately be expected to deviate and give an extra amount of support or rejection to a candidate. In 1960, there was a Catholic candidate and we can see in the Catholic covariation graph that Kennedy received extra support from Catholics. Another unusual divergence came in 2016 when women moved decidedly away from the Republican candidate, Donald Trump. This is easy to explain—Trump was a misogynist. However, in 2016, women did not give extra support to Hillary Clinton.

Unfortunately, the attitude toward candidate data was not available in 2008 or 2012 so there is no comparable covariation data to see the effect of an African-American candidate. However, we can measure the vote itself, not just the attitude toward Barack Obama. In the eight elections before 2008, the Democratic candidate received an average of 93 percent of African-American vote. In 2008, Obama received 99 percent and in 2013, 98 percent of the African-American vote.

The only other instance of non-parallel or non-tandem movement was when class was the demographic. Why was class an outlier, not behaving in the tandem fashion as the other demographic groups? First, let us look at how many middle-class, working-class, and classless voters we are talking about. What class do voters identify with?[1] Since the millennium, about 40 percent identify with the middle class, 30 percent with the working class, and 30 percent feel they belong to no class.[2] We will see later, in Chapter 6, that conservatives tend to identify with the middle class. Thus, an appeal to the middle class will mostly be an appeal to conservatives and it will be directed at only 40 percent of the voters.

Starting in the 1990s, Democratic leaders and candidates usually mentioned only the middle class when making their appeals. We see in the graph of middle and working-class attitudes toward the candidates that this appeal to the middle class by the Democrats worked to a very limited extent; attitudes of the middle class became slightly favorable to Democratic candidates.

Working-class voters, on the other hand, were no longer very positive toward the Democratic candidates. In many elections before the 1990s, especially in 1964 and 1976, working-class attitudes toward Democratic candidates had been very positive. Also, in all elections from 1964 through 1984, there was a gap between attitudes of the working class and middle class—a gap that one would expect given the pro working-class policies of the Democratic Party *at that time*.

By concentrating on the middle class starting in the 1990s, Democratic leaders may have gained a few votes from the middle class, but they have lost their base in the working class and are ignoring those who choose not to be in a class—these two class identifiers make up 60 percent of the electorate.

Red and Blue States

Unfortunately, the publisher of this book does not have the capability of printing in color. It has become customary for political analysts to refer to states that vote Republican as "red" states and those that vote Democratic, as "blue" states. In drawing my maps, I have had to depict state partisanship in black and white. So in this chapter, red states will be colored white and blue states, black. The text in the chapter will use the traditional red and blue terminology, but when referring to maps, red states will be labeled "white" (in parenthesis) and blue will be labeled "black" (in parenthesis).

Short-term forces sweep across the entire country causing similar change in every state. As mentioned earlier, these forces are like the wind and that wind blows across state lines. This can be seen in the change from blue (black) to red (white) or vice versa in many states as we move from election to election. (See Figures 2.5a and 2.5b.) This change can be so sweeping that almost all states turn the same color—a landslide. We noted at the beginning of this chapter that there were landslides in five elections (1964, 1972, 1980, 1984, and 1988) and in these elections almost all states became uniform in color. In most other elections, there is an ever-changing mix of colors as a result of the ever-changing strength and direction of short-term forces. Only nine of the 50 states have never changed color—North Dakota, South Dakota, Idaho, Utah, Wyoming, Kansas, Nebraska, Oklahoma, and Indiana.[3]

The reason why some states are usually blue and some red is due to the distribution of party identifiers in each state. Some states have a disproportionate number of Democrats, while others have a disproportionate number of Republicans. The likelihood of a state turning colors in a particular election depends on the how disparate these proportions are. States that have nearly equal proportions of Democrats and Republicans could change colors with even a slight asymmetry in short-term forces. These will be called "Toss-up" states.[4] The reason why the nine states mentioned above have never changed is because they have an unusually large number of Republican residents.

The only way for the proportions of Republicans and Democrats in a state to change is through conversion or migration. There was conversion in the South in the 1960s (discussed in Chapter 1) in which a great many Southerners changed from Democrat to Independent or Republican. That can be seen by comparing the 1960 map with the 1964 map. The South has been all red (white) in most elections since then.

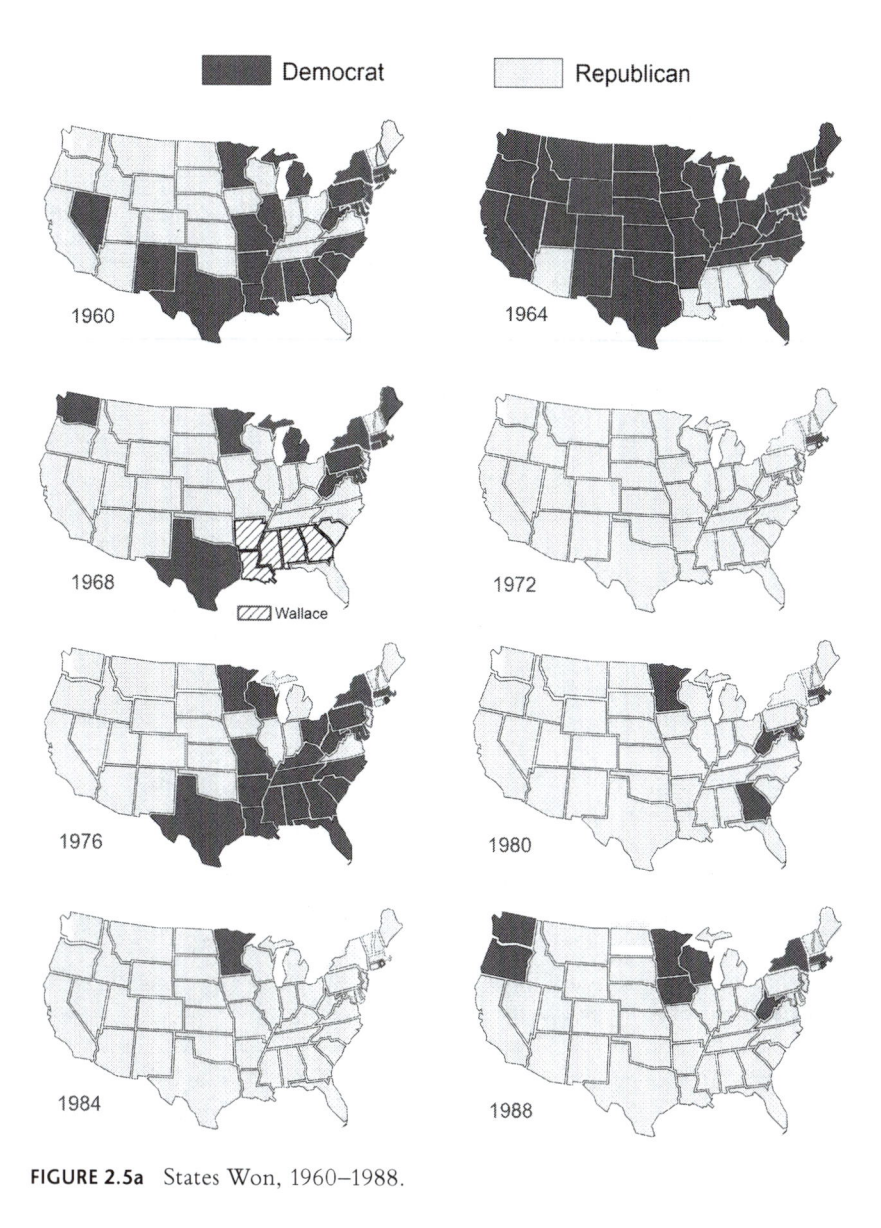

FIGURE 2.5a States Won, 1960–1988.

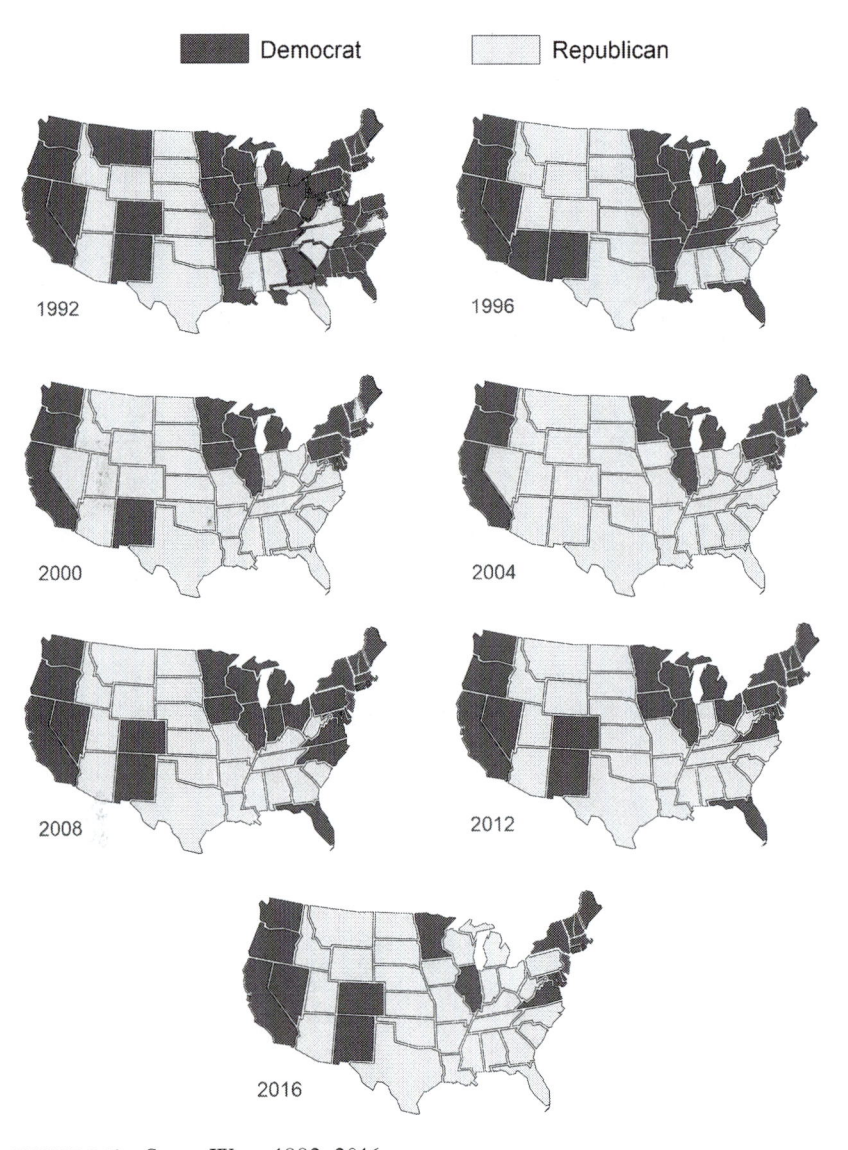

Democrat   **Republican**

1992   1996
2000   2004
2008   2012
2016

FIGURE 2.5b States Won, 1992–2016.

Change in the coloration of a state can also be due to migration—a disproportionate number of Republican or Democratic identifiers moving into or out of a state. For example, Virginia changed from red to Toss-up due to the unusual number of Democrats who moved to the Northern Virginia areas around Washington, DC.

There are occasional aberrations in the vote of some states that are not due to short-term forces. This is a result of the favorite-son phenomenon. Barry

Goldwater was from Arizona, which stayed red (white) when most of the rest of the country turned blue (black). Jimmy Carter was a Southerner (from Georgia); note that the Southern states suddenly turned blue (black) in 1976. In 1968, the former Alabama governor, George Wallace, ran as an independent. He won the Deep South (shown in hashed lines in the Electoral Map that year). Also, note that Minnesota, the home state of Walter Mondale, was the only blue (black) state in 1984.

The Steady State of the States

It would be helpful in predicting the Electoral College vote if we could measure the normal vote in each state—the "steady state" of each state. Knowing that "steady state," we could estimate how strong the short-term forces would have to be in order to change the state's color (not permanently, but in that election). To estimate this normal vote of states requires estimating the proportions of Republicans and Democrats in each state. Unfortunately, finding the proportions of Republicans and Democrats in each state is very difficult. There are few reliable state-wide sample surveys in which party identification is obtained. Registration does not work since many states do not require voters to give their party affiliation. Therefore, one has to use surrogate data.

One of the measures I used to estimate the normal vote of states was to look at the vote for down-ticket offices in state elections—offices such as attorney general or secretary of state. Votes for these offices are often party-line votes. Also, voting patterns for presidents over *many years* can help to see the partisan orientation of the state. Using these measures, I produced a map showing how states would vote if there were no short-term forces—the normal vote or steady state of each state (Figure 2.6).

Although most of the country looks Republican, this is due to the fact that a good part of the country consists of sparsely populated states in the mid-west and west. There is a total of 178 Electoral Votes in Republican states; the Democrats have 154—a fairly even split.

There are also twelve Toss-up states that could go either way with just a very small push from short-term forces. Note, for example, that Barack Obama took all of the Toss-up states in 2012 with just a one percent margin of victory nationwide. Trump took only six of the twelve Toss-up states when short-term forces countered each other in 2016. Much stronger forces would be necessary to cause a deep red or a deep blue state to change colors in an election. For example, in the 2018 off-year election there were very strong anti-Trump forces as indicated by the forty-seat increase in Democratic congressmen (the so-called blue wave). This strong wave also affected Senate races. Eleven deep red states were holding Senate races in 2018; the Democrats won three of them (Arizona, Montana, and West Virginia).

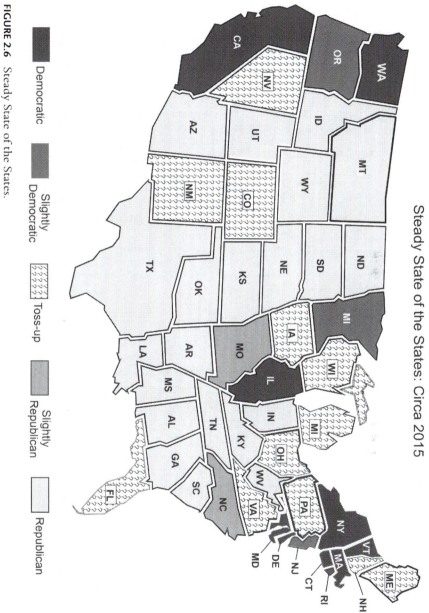

Steady State of the States: Circa 2015

Democratic

Slightly
Democratic

Toss-up

Slightly
Republican

Republican

FIGURE 2.6 Steady State of the States.

The twelve Toss-up states have a total of 140 Electoral Votes. They are in almost every region of the country so there is no way to tailor appeals to all of them. An appeal to just some could be counter-productive since that would leave out, or even offend, the remainder of these potential votes. Barry Goldwater tried this in 1964 with his "Southern Strategy." His strategy did work and he won the South, but lost the rest of the country. Five of the Toss-up states are in the Rust Belt (Pennsylvania, Ohio, Michigan, Iowa, and Wisconsin.) and Trump did win these states with his anti-free trade and anti-outsourcing positions. But those positions did not offend the rest of the country and Trump won many other states for other reasons.

Furthermore, there is no point in making a special appeal to the Toss-up states (even if that were possible given their variety). Short-term forces sweep across the entire country. The objective of any campaign should be to have the short-term forces blowing in your direction by having a strong candidate and addressing the concerns of the Issue Publics which, as we will see, are usually concerned with national problems. That strategy would win all or almost all of the Toss-up states and many more.

The Steady State of the States map presented here will probably be useful for another ten years, but after that it will have to be revisited. Migration of party identifiers either into or out of certain states could change their coloration.

Notes

1 Social scientists often use demographic characteristics, such as income and education, to place a voter in a class. The voter does not know he or she is in that class. The class the voter himself or herself chooses to identify with is the class that could influence their vote. When candidates make their appeal explicitly to the middle class, those listeners who identify with the working class will not think the candidate is addressing them.
2 Class identity is based on the ANES question "Do you think of yourself as belonging to a class?" and if "yes" "which class, middle or working?"
3 Even these nine states turned blue in 1964.
4 I do not call these "swing" states since that implies that they are regularly going back and forth as one does on a swing. Remember, each election starts de novo with a normal vote that is based on the relative proportions of Republicans and Democrats— proportions that do not change readily. Per chance, short-term forces could move a state in one partisan direction twice, or even three elections in a row. It would remain a "Toss-up" state if the distribution of party identifiers remained the same.

Reference

Converse, Philip. 1966. *Elections and the Political Order*, chap 2. New York: John Wiley and Sons.

3

MEASURING ISSUES

In the Introduction we saw that issues measured with pre-selected, pre-formulated, fixed-choice (closed-ended) questions do not have an effect on vote. Hundreds of such questions were entered into the Model Equation, one at a time, and almost none had any significant weight in voters' decisions. This should not come as a surprise for three basic reasons: (1) the questions are based on issues that the political elite are discussing—issues that are not necessarily those that ordinary voters are concerned with, (2) voters cannot possibly pay attention to and develop an attitude toward all of the dozens of issues presented to them in a poll, and (3) if a voter does not have an attitude toward the issue, he or she responds anyway, perhaps because they do not want to appear uninformed or because there is a word or phrase in the question they do have an attitude toward. As we shall see, the majority of responses to closed-ended questions are guesses.

The results of an issue poll are often called either an "opinion" or an "attitude"; the terms are used interchangeably. I believe that it is important to make a distinction between an attitude and an opinion. An "attitude" is defined in the social psychological literature as a *predisposition* to respond in a particular way to an object. It is something a person has given at least some thought to and is stored in memory. I define "opinion" (as in "public opinion") as the response given to a question—a "gut reaction" to the words presented to the respondent. An attitude is something the respondent has in mind both before and after an interview, an opinion is a reaction to a question that the respondent may never have thought about before an interview nor will think about again when the interview is over. The results of polls should be called "polled reactions" in order to avoid the false impression that poll questions measure attitudes. It also serves to remind us that "public opinion" would not exist unless there were polls.

Attempts to Measure Real Attitudes with Closed Questions

Following are some examples of the hundreds of times closed-ended questions have led to highly unreliable and meaningless findings:[1]

> In a *Washington Post* survey, respondents were asked their opinion about a non-existent Public Affairs Act. Forty-three percent gave an opinion.

In a NORC (National Opinion Research Center) study, respondents were asked "I'm going to name some problems and for each one I'd like you to tell me whether too much, too little, or about the right amount is being spent on them?" One sample was asked about spending for "assistance to the poor" and another sample was asked about spending for "welfare." Sixth-three percent of the first sample thought we were spending "too little" on the "poor," but only 23 percent of those in the second sample said we were spending "too little" on "welfare." Respondents' prior attitudes toward those on "welfare" and those who are poor obviously triggered the different reactions to these questions. Wording of the question is vital.

In a sample of voting sites across the country in 2004, voters were given a questionnaire as they left the voting station (the Exit Poll). Voters were asked to choose from a pre-selected list of seven issues—"which one issue mattered most in deciding how you voted for president?" "Moral values" was one of the items on the list. It was the most frequently selected issue—22 percent selected it. A few days later, the Pew Research Center for the People and the Press conducted a split-sample survey in which one half were given the question as it had appeared in the Exit Poll, and the other half was asked the same question as an open-ended one (with no list of issues). In the Pew experiment, 27 percent of the sample that had been administered the Exit Poll list picked the "moral values" option, while "moral values" was on the minds of only 14 percent as an open-ended response. As a result of the Exit Poll, most political analysts concluded (erroneously) that the main issue in 2004 was moral values. The Exit Poll respondents had been given a prompt (a list) that triggered an answer. But most voters in the country had not been given a list and voted what was on their minds.

In addition, researchers sometimes conceptualize issues very differently than the average voter and thus frame questions in ways that respondents have never thought about. During the Vietnam War, for example, the ANES asked:

> Which of the following do you think we should do now in Vietnam? Pull out of Vietnam entirely, keep our soldiers in Vietnam but try to end the fighting, or take a stronger stand even if it means invading North Vietnam?

Most respondents picked one of the options yet had no idea what our military strategy should be. We know they had no idea since before being asked this fixed-choice question, respondents had been asked the open-ended Most Important Problem question. A great many mentioned the war in Vietnam as a problem, and most of them wanted it to end *but did not know how.* Some typical comments were: "I really don't know. I don't want to see them pull out but I don't know what should be done." "I would like to see peace but I wouldn't know what the solution would be." "Settle it and get it over with." "Try to stop it. Get it over with." "I'd like to see it ended honorably with both sides giving in enough to create a peace." This is a case where the political elite (the researchers) conceptualized the issue of Vietnam in strategic terms. This question asked ordinary citizens to make a decision that only political experts and generals could answer. If researchers wanted to find the public's opinion about the war, they should have asked, simply, "was the war a mistake or not?"

Another example of asking the public questions that they could not possibly answer is the following (asked by a Gallup/CNN/*USA Today* poll during the war in Iraq):

> As you may know, elections will be held in Iraq early next year. Which comes closest to your view—the election will not produce a stable democratic government in Iraq, the elections will produce a stable democratic government in Iraq, but the U.S. will need to keep the same number of troops it has there for at least another year, or the elections will produce a stable democratic government in Iraq and the U.S. will be able to significantly reduce the number of troops it has there within the next year?

Perhaps a joint committee of State Department and Defense Department officials could begin to answer this question. Why ask the public?

Some question formats try to screen out those who are not familiar with the issue by adding the following phrase to the question "or haven't you thought about it." Another method to screen out guessers that has been tried is to ask "how important is this to you" after the respondent has answered the basic question. Neither method gets rid of enough guessers to make the remaining answers real attitudes. The positions taken on these screened questions still do not correlate with vote.

Testing for the Extent of Random Response

There is need for a method of measuring how many respondents are responding randomly—for finding out how reliable the question is. I have discovered such a method using test–retest data. When the same respondents are surveyed at two successive times, these studies are known as panels. The ANES has executed several two-wave panels over the years. These test–retest studies allow us

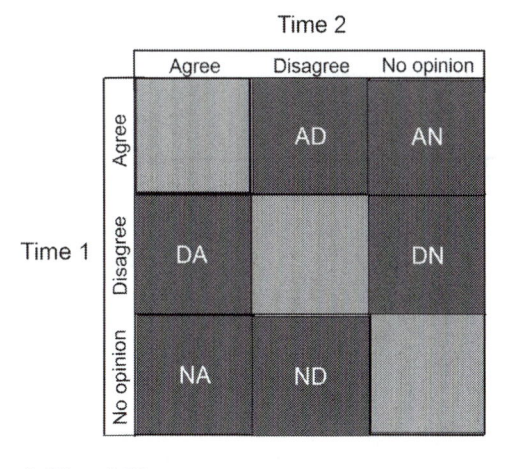

FIGURE 3.1 Time 1–Time 2 Figure.

to see how much turnover there is in response to closed-ended panel questions. Turnover is a strong indication of guessing—of non-attitudes.[2]

Figure 3.1 depicts the cells of a cross-tabulation of fixed-choice answers at Time 1 and Time 2. Those cases that fall into the black cells have changed their answers. For example, cases in cell AD have gone from Agree to Disagree and cases in cell AN have gone from Agree to No Opinion. Because they have changed, almost all those in the black cells can be considered random responders. Those in the gray cells have answered the same way twice, indicating stability and thus a real attitude. The problem is that some respondents in these gray cells could have been guessing but nonetheless given the same answer twice just by chance; in essence, they flipped a coin and came up with heads twice or tails twice. How many respondents in the gray cells are random responders and how many were consistent because they have an attitude? This problem has plagued opinion researchers for many years.

I have discovered a way to estimate how many random responders are there in the gray cells. The results can be seen in Table 3.1, which shows the proportion of random responders to questions in the ANES panels. (A detailed explanation of my method of finding random responders can be found in Appendix B.)

Most of the questions elicited high proportions of random responses. *In twenty-six of the thirty-one questions tested, over half of the respondents answered randomly; often as many as 60–70 percent were random responders.* Only five questions elicited fairly stable responses, indicating that most of those respondents had real attitudes. Most of these were questions about moral issues (the death penalty and abortion), issues that are often based on long-term religious beliefs.

It is interesting to note that it made no difference how much time had passed between the first interview and the second. Some questions were asked in the pre-election interview and repeated in the post-election interview—a time

TABLE 3.1 Amount of Random Response

ANES Data Source		Estimated % of Random Response
1990–92 Panel	Favor or oppose *death penalty* for murder	33
1990–92 Panel	Position on *abortion*: four choices ranging from never permitted to personal choice	34
1980 Pre-Post	Position on *abortion*: four choices ranging from never permitted to personal choice	34
08–09 Panel	*Raising income tax* on those making over $200,000 a year	44
2008–09 Panel	U.S. government pay for all the cost of *prescription drugs for low income seniors*	45
1980 Panel	Less money for defense or increase *defense spending*	50
2008–09 Panel	U.S. *government pay for all necessary medical care* for all Americans	51
2008–09 Panel	Make it *possible for illegal immigrants to become U.S. citizens*	53
2008–09 Panel	Require government to get a *court order to tap phone calls* of suspected terrorists	56
1956–58 Panel	Government in Washington give *money to cities and towns to build more schools*	56
1956–58 Panel	Government should see to it that *Negroes get fair treatment in jobs and housing*	57
2008–09 Panel	Constitutional amendment to *ban gay marriage*	58
2008–09 Panel	Allow government to *imprison suspected terrorists without charge* or bringing to court	58
2008–09 Panel	Allow *illegal immigrants to work in U.S. for up to 3 years* before sending them back	58
1956–58 Panel	Government in Washington should see to it that *everybody can find a job*	59
1956–58 Panel	This country should *just stay home* and not concern ourselves with the world	59
2004 Pre-Post	*Solve international problems* with diplomacy rather than military force	62
1972–74 Panel	*Equal role for women* or women's place in the home	63
1976 Pre-Post	Government see to it that *every person has a job* or just let get ahead on their own	63
1984 Pre-Post	Government should *provide fewer services* like health and education or provide more	64
1956–58 Panel	*Keep soldiers overseas* to help countries that are against communism	64
1990–92 Panel	Less money for defense or increase *defense spending*	65
1956–58 Panel	Government in Washington stay out of *white and colored going to same school*	66

(Continued)

ANES Data Source		Estimated % of Random Response
1984 Pre-Post	Government see to it that *every person has a job* or just let get ahead on their own	68
1972–74 Panel	Government *improve social and economic position of* *blacks* or help themselves	69
1980 Panel	*Try to get along with Russia* or mistake to try	70
1990–92 Panel	Government *improve social and economic position of* *blacks* or help themselves	71
1990–92 Panel	Government see to it that *every person has a job* or just let get ahead on their own	72
1956–58 Panel	Government should leave *electric power and* *housing* to private businessmen	73
1990–92 Panel	Government should *provide fewer services* like health and education or provide more	74
1956–58 Panel	The United States should give *economic help to* *the poorer countries*	77

interval of just one or two months. The questions from the 1980 panel were asked five months apart (January and June). Many questions shown in Table 3.1 were separated by an interval of two years. Yet the turnover results were about the same for the same questions regardless of time interval.

Any issue that has over 50 percent random response is one that most respondents have not thought about, or perhaps even heard of, before the interview. The data in Table 3.1 demonstrate that the phenomenon of random response is real and observable and is endemic in almost all closed-ended issue questions. The only way to learn which issues voters are concerned with and have an attitude toward is to use open-ended questions. With these questions, there are no words to prompt an answer or for respondents to react to. An issue that is mentioned in response to an open-ended question must have been in mind before the interview or else there would be no response at all.

Issue Publics

"Issue Publics" are all those voters who have an attitude toward an issue. The way to find these Issue Publics is through the use of open-ended questions. An Issue Public is not a group—not something people join. Rather it is simply all those individuals who, separately and on their own, have become concerned about an issue. An Issue Public may be as small as 2 percent of voters or as large as 75 or 80 percent. An individual can be in several Issue Publics at the same time if he or she is concerned with more than one issue.

As we saw in the Introduction, the open-ended question used to measure Issue Publics is "what are the most important problems facing the country." Up to three problems were recorded by the ANES interviewers. (Almost all voters had at least one issue in mind; on average, they were concerned with 2.5 issues.) Respondents were then asked which of the problems they had mentioned was the "single most important." In order to measure the partisan direction, the respondent attached to that issue, the respondent was then asked, "which party do you think will do a better job in dealing with the problem—the Republicans, the Democrats, or wouldn't there be much difference between them?"

Table 3.2 shows the Issue Publics in elections since 1960.

TABLE 3.2 Issue Publics 1960–2016

Issue Public	MIP	Issue	Party to Deal with the Problem			
			Net Effect	Dem	No Diff or DK	Rep
		1960				
16.3	7.5	Unemployment, poor economy	55D	64%	27	9	100%
20.1	5.9	Farm problems, crop payments, surpluses		35%	33	32	100%
11.0	3.7	Problems of the aged, need for medical care	19D	48%	23	29	100%
14.0	2.8	Integration (either pro/con or neutral)	13D	28%	56	15	100%
	13.3	Other domestic issues		36%	38	26	100%
	33.2%	Total Domestic				
25.8	19.8	Cold war; general concern with war and peace	13R	26%	35	39	100%
26.6	16.9	More defense spending, firm stand against USSR	13R	30%	27	43	100%
18.3	11.8	Negotiate with USSR, build better relations		25%	41	34	100%
7.8	3.9	Cuba, takeover by Castro	15R	22%	41	37	100%
	8.9	Other foreign and defense		32%	41	27	100%
	61.3%	Total Foreign and Defense				
		1964				
13.5	7.5	Pro civil rights, pro-integration	67D	71%	25	4	100%
10.6	5.9	Civil rights generally (no position taken)	34D	45%	44	11	100%
16.5	7.7	Problems of the aged, Medicare	62D	69%	24	7	100%
9.5	5.3	Unemployment	42D	56%	30	14	100%
8.6	3.2	Poverty, problems of the poor	55D	61%	33	8	100%
	23.8	Other domestic issues		26%	36	38	100%
	53.4%	Total Domestic				

(*Continued*)

			Party to Deal with the Problem			
Issue Public	MIP	Issue	Net Effect	Dem	No Diff or DK	Rep

1964 (Continued)

Issue Public	MIP	Issue	Net Effect	Dem	No Diff or DK	Rep
5.4	3.4	Strong defense, firm stand against USSR		32%	29	39	100%
4.6	3.3	Cold War, general concern with war and peace	52D	60%	32	8	100%
5.1	3.2	Relations with USSR, generally		33%	39	28	100%
16.2	7.8	Vietnam		28%	36	36	100%
	11.7	Other foreign and defense		38%	31	31	100%
	37.9%	Total Foreign and Defense					

1968

Issue Public	MIP	Issue	Net Effect	Dem	No Diff or DK	Rep
27.6	11.4	Riots, public disorder	28R	12%	43	40	100%
20.9	5.5	Poverty, Great Society	34D	49%	36	15	100%
15.9	5.0	Civil rights generally, no position taken)	25D	41%	43	16	100%
7.9	2.9	Pro civil rights, integration					
7.4	3.6	War protests, demonstrations		7%	64	14	100%
	20.2	Other domestic issues		23%	44	33	100%
	48.6%	Total Domestic					
69.8	42.8	Vietnam	13R	21%	45	34	100%
	6.6	Other foreign and defense	23R	10%	57	33	100%
	49.4%	Total Foreign and Defense					

1972

Issue Public	MIP	Issue	Net Effect	Dem	No Diff or DK	Rep
26.0	12.7	Inflation		27%	51	22	100%
21.4	8.3	Unemployment, the economy	31R	18%	42	49	100%
8.5	5.2	Moral decay		15%	70	15	100%
13.0	4.9	Drugs		21%	69	10	100%
17.6	4.4	Civil rights generally (no position taken)	13R	20%	46	33	100%
9.3	4.2	Crime	13D	29%	56	16	100%
7.9	2.7	Poverty, welfare		21%	46	32	100%
	23.0	Other domestic issues		28%	50	22	100%
	65.4%	Total domestic issues					
43.5	25.1	Vietnam	13D	34%	45	21	100%
	9.5	Other foreign and defense		25%	45	30	100%
	34.6%	Total Foreign and defense					

			Party to Deal with the Problem			
Issue Public	MIP	Issue	Net Effect	Dem	No Diff or DK	Rep
			1976			
56.2	28.2	Unemployment	53D	57%	39	4	100%
47.5	26.3	Inflation		29%	47	24	100%
16.8	9.9	The economy generally		33%	45	22	100%
15.2	4.8	Crime, violence		19%	71	10	100%
17.1	4.0	Fuel shortages, energy crisis	27D	31%	65	4	100%
	17.4	Other domestic issues		24%	60	18	100%
	90.6%	Total domestic issues					
	4.1	All Foreign and defense		14%	66	20	100%
			1980			
55.6	36.7	Inflation	48R	8%	36	56	100%
29.1	8.4	Unemployment		16%	56	28	100%
	21.4	Other domestic issues		14%	50	36	100%
	66.5%	Total Domestic issues					
25.4	13.9	Hostages in Iran	23R	12%	53	35	100%
25.3	8.9	Strong defense, increase defense budget	59R	5%	31	64	100%
7.0	3.1	Prevent war, for disarmament		26%	44	30	100%
	5.4	Other foreign and defense		4%	28	68	100%
	31.3%	Total Foreign and Defense					
			1984			
39.3	21.4	Budget deficit	18R	21%	40	39	100%
33.3	15.7	Unemployment, the economy		32%	40	28	100%
8.5	4.0	Inflation	26R	13%	48	39	100%
7.2	1.7	Poverty, welfare programs generally	17D	39%	39	22	100%
4.8	1.8	Help the poor, increase social welfare	60D	60%	40	0	100%
	17.3	Other domestic issues	17R	21%	40	38	100%
	62.9%	Total Domestic					
35.6	19.1	Threat of nuclear war, end arms race		32%	42	26	100%
8.9	3.7	Against détente, maintain military strength	78R	2%	18	80	100%
5.7	2.1	Relations with USSR, for détente	34R	21%	24	55	100%
8.0	2.6	Nicaragua		26%	43	39	100%
	5.0	Other foreign and defense	19R	20%	41	39	100%
	32.5%	Total Foreign and Defense					

(*Continued*)

Issue			Party to Deal with the Problem			
Public	MIP	Issue	Net Effect	Dem	No Diff or DK	Rep

1988

47.6	33.4	Budget deficit, national debt	16R	16%	52	32	100%
15.4	6.0	Unemployment	36D	50%	36	14	100%
15.9	4.9	Environment, clean air	20D	23%	74	3	100%
30.0	4.2	Drugs, interdiction, drug-related crimes		18%	66	16	100%
13.6	3.4	The homeless	46D	53%	40	7	100%
10.2	3.2	Poverty, aid to poor	29D	40%	49	11	100%
12.7	3.1	Foreign trade, limit Imports, outsourcing		28%	42	30	100%
4.9	3.0	Moral decay of country, family values	31R	9%	51	40	100%
7.5	2.6	Education	17D	40%	37	23	100%
	<u>14.5</u>	Other domestic issues		32%	43	25	100%
	87.3%	Total Domestic issues					
12.7	3.1	Foreign trade, limit imports, outsourcing		28%	42	30	100%
8.9	2.7	Prevent war, disarmament, SALT	35R	6%	53	41	100%
	<u>4.7</u>	Other foreign and defense		29%	40	31	100%
	10.5%	Other Foreign and Defense					

1992

60.1	37.3	Unemployment, the economy	41D	49%	43	8	100%
17.5	12.4	National debt, government spending		28%	49	23	100%
18.6	5.2	Health insurance	48D	55%	40	5	100%
7.8	4.3	Moral decay of country, lack of family values	36R	9%	39	52	100%
12.5	3.5	Drugs, drug-related violence		22%	64	14	100%
12.3	2.7	Welfare, aid to dependent children (ADC)	33D	42%	49	9	100%
9.0	2.6	Crime		12%	75	14	100%
10.7	2.5	Education	44D	56%	39	5	100%
	<u>13.6</u>	Other domestic issues					
	90.1%	Total domestic					
	4.7%	Foreign and Defense					

Issue Public	MIP	Issue	Party to Deal with the Problem			
			Net Effect	Dem	No Diff or DK	Rep

1996

Issue Public	MIP	Issue	Net Effect	Dem	No Diff or DK	Rep
36.6	15.9	Drugs, crime, violence in streets	14R	9%	68	23	100%
22.4	13.3	Balancing the budget, national debt	25R	10%	55	35	100%
36.1	10.9	Welfare, ADC	18D	37%	44	19	100%
15.7	9.7	Moral decay of country, lack of family values	33R	7%	53	40	100%
19.7	8.7	Education	55D	65%	25	10	100%
9.9	8.5	The economy, unemployment		31%	49	20	100%
15.5	5.8	Medical care, health insurance	35D	41%	53	6	100%
	20.5	Other domestic issues		29%	37	34	100%
	93.3%	Total Domestic issues					
	4.9%	Foreign and Defense					

2000

Issue Public	MIP	Issue	Net Effect	Dem	No Diff or DK	Rep
32.6	16.1	Education	23D	44%	35	21	100%
17.3	10.9	Moral decay of country, lack of family values	32R	10%	48	42	100%
22.2	8.8	Medical care, health insurance	42D	48%	46	6	100%
23.1	8.4	Social Security, prescription drugs	13D	36%	41	23	100%
16.1	6.5	Drugs, drug-related violence		14%	61	25	100%
9.6	4.9	The economy unemployment	14D	44%	26	30	100%
11.2	3.5	Welfare, ADC	16D	16%	84	0	100%
6.3	3.0	Balancing the budget, national debt	27R	20%	33	47	100%
	23.2	Other domestic issues		27%	41	32	100%
	85.3%	Total Domestic issues					
9.6	3.0	Increase defense budget	81R	0%	19	81	100%
	8.9	Other foreign and defense		18%	54	28	100%
	11.9%	Total Foreign and defense					

2004

Issue Public	MIP	Issue				
	41.6	Terrorism	Only one issue recorded			
	18.4	Iraq war	Party to best handle was not asked			
	13.2	The economy, unemployment				

(Continued)

Issue			Party to Deal with the Problem			
Public	MIP	Issue	Net Effect	Dem	No Diff or DK	Rep

2008

50.4	38.8	The economy				
38.2	15.1	War, Iraq, Middle East				
14.5	5.9	Employment, jobs				
8.6	5.4	Partisan politics, politicians, government in general	Party to best handle was not asked			
9.2	4.8	International affairs				
10.3	3.3	Terrorism				

2016

42.2	19.2	Economy, need jobs that pay, outsourcing	17R	24%	35	41	100%
21.8	12.2	Divisiveness, hatred between groups	42D	49%	44	7	100%
20.4	9.4	Racism, police treatment, "Black Lives Matter"	57D	66%	25	9	100%
18.0	5.9	Immigration, protect borders	43R	20%	18	63	100%
16.3	5.7	Health care		31%	33	36	100%
13.5	5.6	Terrorism and ISIS	17R	25%	32	42	100%
9.6	3.5	Income gap, rich get richer	67D	67%	33	0	100%
8.3	3.9	Global warming, environment	29D	33%	63	4	100%
8.0	4.1	National debt	41R	7%	45	48	100%
7.8	3.2	Poverty, homelessness		38%	38	24	100%
6.7	3.0	The newly elected president, Donald Trump	75D	75%	25	0	100%
	_12.1_	Other domestic issues		34%	35	31	100%
	87.6%	Total Domestic				
17.7	6.4	Foreign affairs, relations with other countries	15D	46%	23	31	100%
	_2.2_	Defense				
	8.6%	Total Foreign and Defense				

The tables list only those Issue Publics that were of sufficient size to have contributed significantly to the election outcome. To be listed in this table, the issue must have been brought up by at least 7 percent of voters and must have been the single most important issue for at least 3 percent. These may seem so small that they are insignificant, but any one of them could spell the difference between winning and losing in those elections which are decided by only a small margin such as 1960, 1976, 1996, 2000, 2004, 2012, and 2016.

There are many Issue Publics of less than 7 percent—too small to be listed separately. These tiny Issue Publics, when added up, amount to about 20 percent of the electorate. However, the net partisan effect of these Issue Publics is nil; about equal numbers of respondents named issues that they thought the Republicans could handle as named issues that the Democrats could handle, and there were many issues that neither party was seen as able to handle.

The History of Important Problems

The data in the Issue Publics table (3.2) *reveal an unfolding history as recorded in the minds of voters.* Throughout much of the period under study, the threat of a nuclear war with the USSR hung over the country. Issue Publics regarding relations with the USSR and defense were present in most elections until 1989 when the Cold War ended and the Berlin Wall was torn down.

Cuba had been taken over by Fidel Castro in 1959 and Cuba was an issue in 1960. The 1960s were one of the most tumultuous in American history. Southern laws that required segregation of blacks and denied their civil rights brought on the Civil Rights Movement, which used non-violent civil disobedience to bring attention to these Jim Crow laws. The activities of the Civil Rights Movement became highly visible starting in 1961. For example, television news showed the beatings received by freedom riders. There were pictures of lunch counter sit-ins where blacks were refused service. Three voter registration workers were murdered. Martin Luther King, Jr. gave his well-known "I Have a Dream Speech" at the Lincoln Memorial in 1963. Not surprisingly, a large civil rights Issue Public emerged in the 1964 election.

President Johnson began sending U.S. troops to Vietnam soon after the 1964 election and he kept sending more and more. The war was shown every night on the news. By the time of the 1968 election, many thousands of American troops had been killed and the end was not in sight. Seventy percent of the voters cited the Vietnam War as an issue in 1968.

At the same time, the ongoing discrimination against and suppression of blacks (such as segregation, police harassment, bad schools and job discrimination)[3] sparked racial riots. These riots started in 1965 in Watts (Los Angeles), followed by riots in many cities such as Newark, Minneapolis, Chicago, Washington, and most notably, Detroit in 1967. During these riots, there were spectacular scenes of whole blocks being burned down. The assassination of Martin Luther King, Jr. in April 1968 caused further disturbances in many cities. Very large Issue Publics formed around the problem of rioting in 1968.

The Vietnam War continued after 1968 and anti-war sentiment became especially intense in 1970 when pictures of Vietnamese women and children being massacred in Mai Lai were shown on all media. At that time, the war was expanded by invading Cambodia. There were demonstrations and sit-ins on many college campuses resulting in national guard troops being called to restore order. Four students were killed and nine wounded by Ohio national guard troops at Kent State. The ongoing war in Vietnam and its consequences remained as a major issue in 1972.

The economy was also a major issue in some of the election years between 1960 and 2016, especially the rampant inflation in the late 1970s and the Great Recession in 2008. (The issue of the economy will be discussed in detail later in the chapter.)

Issue Publics formed around a variety of other problems in the 1960–2016 period. There were fuel shortages in the 1970s and the drug problem was first mentioned in 1972 and reemerged in 1988, 1992 1996, and 2000. It was top issue in 1996. Health care began to make the MIP lists in 1992 and remained on the list thereafter. The national debt and failure to balance the budget topped the list in 1984, 1988, 1992, 1996 and remained on the list (at a lower level) in 2000 and 2016. The environment made it onto the list of Issue Publics in 1988 and global warming in 2016. The gap in wealth with a few at the top owning a very large portion of the wealth became an issue in 2016.

Other well-publicized problems also became visible from time to time. Starting in 1979. American Embassy employees had been held hostage in Iran and were still there during the 1980 election period. The clandestine shipment of arms to Nicaraguan insurgents (the Iran–Contra scandal) was revealed in 1986 and was an issue in the 1988 election.

In summary, the major events and conditions in the period of this study were the principal source of concern of the electorate and Issue Publics formed around them.

The Unexpected Findings

Other major issue concerns were unexpected. They had seldom been in the news and were issues that were seldom discussed by candidates in the campaigns. Education was near the top of the list from 1988 onward; in 2000 it topped the list. The "moral decay of country" was first mentioned by the public in 1972 and was on the list in 1988, 1992, 1996 and 2000.[4] Problems of the aged first appeared in 1960 and 1964, but ended after Medicare was established in the 1965. Homelessness was of considerable concern in 1988 and 2016; affordable housing was an issue in 1992.

Issues that have been prominent in political discourse but have never had Issue Public form around them are gun control, school prayer, and issues regarding homosexuals. The women's movement, which was especially strong in the 1970s with the push for an Equal Rights Amendment, received almost no mention.

In sum, it is very difficult to predict or anticipate all the problems that will draw large numbers of voters into an Issue Public. Just because an issue is widely discussed in elite circles, and given a lot of attention by the media, does not mean that it is of concern to many ordinary citizens.

Abortion and Taxes

Perhaps most surprising are two issues that have never made it onto the list of Issue Publics. For decades, abortion and taxes have been "litmus test" issues for Republican candidates. Whenever the Republicans gain a majority in Congress, they immediately get to work to limit abortions and adamantly refuse to raise taxes. Yet never in the five and a half decades of this study were abortion and taxes ever mentioned as an important issue. The Republican Party positions on these issues clearly do not stem from the concerns of the public. Republicans must be responding to special interests and segments of activists.

General Conclusions about Issues

The following general conclusions can be drawn from the Issue Publics Tables:

Reality, not rhetoric. Most often the issue concerns of the public stem *not* from the discussion and the rhetoric of political elites but from real events, actual conditions, or clearly evident problems. These include daily news of events such as war, personal experience with high prices during an inflationary period, seeing unemployment among neighbors and friends or becoming unemployed oneself, and reports on the size of the federal debt produce Issue Publics. Public concern about civil rights was a result of a highly visible movement lead by Martin Luther King, Jr. Rioting by blacks and the burning of their communities in the 1960s resulted in a large Issue Public. Issue Publics also formed around other clearly evident problems such as fuel shortages, drugs, and the environment.

There were, however, a few problems that came to the public's attention from discussion among the political elite, policy proposals by candidates, or legislation. For example, Lyndon Johnson's concern for the poor can be seen among the list of Issue Publics in 1964. (This resulted in the Great Society legislation.) Ronald Reagan's arms buildup, along with his strained relations with the "evil empire," revived concern with Cold War issues in 1984. Sizable Issue Publics have developed regarding the issue of health care.

The 2016 election was a major departure from the general rule that issues raised by candidates seldom have developed into Issue Publics. Trump's deriding of non-whites, foreigners, and women created a divisive atmosphere that appalled a large number of Americans as can be seen by the Issue Publics near the top of the 2016 list. People were very concerned with the divisiveness that Trump's rhetoric engendered. Trump also raised concern about immigration—an issue that had never been mentioned before. He, himself, was also considered a problem.

Motivation for the Formation of Issue Publics: Concern for Others or Personal Self-interest?

Personal self-interest hardly ever plays a role in deciding which issues people become concerned about. An average of 70 percent of those concerned about the economy report that their personal financial situation is the same or better. Those who mentioned poverty are mostly *not* low income. Half of those concerned with education did not have children. The issue of civil rights was a concern of a large number of voters in 1964—68 percent were white. Half of those concerned with racism in 2016 were white. Seventy-nine percent of those concerned with farm problems in 1960 were not farmers.

In 1992, respondents were asked, "Can you and your family afford to pay for health care?" Forty-seven percent said they could not afford it. One would expect that these would be the people most concerned about the issue of health care insurance. In fact, more of those who said they *could* afford health care named health care as an important issue.

Other examples of concern for others were "the environment" and "the moral decay of the country." In several years, a sizable Issue Public was concerned with homelessness, although none of these respondents could possibly have been homeless themselves. (The primary sampling units in ANES samples are blocks of dwellings.)

The sole example of personal interest arose in 1964 when a bare majority (52 percent) of the Issue Public concerned with problems of the aged were older than 50 years.

The Economy

The economy is *not* always a major factor in every election. Looking at the Issues Tables, we see that the economic issue (defined as unemployment, inflation or both) was one of the top concerns in only eight of the thirteen elections studied.

Perceived Party Differences

When political parties (or candidates) offer a clear solution to a problem and/or have a history of dealing effectively with it, the Issue Public is aware of party differences. The Issues Tables reveal that Democrats are seen as much better than Republicans at dealing with problems of poverty, homelessness, education, and health insurance, as well as promoting civil rights. Since 1992, the Democrats have also been seen as the environmental protection party. Republicans are seen as much better at dealing with two issues: the moral decay of the country and need for defense spending.

Issue Publics concerned with crime, drugs, and fuel shortages in the 1970s saw no difference between the parties' ability to deal with these problems. Interestingly, the Republican Party was seen as somewhat more likely to deal with the national debt even though debt had increased rapidly under Republican presidents. Even in 2000, the Republicans had a net advantage of twenty-seven points over the Democrats on the budget issue even though a Democratic president (Clinton) had achieved a surplus in his last years in office.[5]

Before 1980, in elections in which "unemployment" was high on the list of issues, Democrats were always viewed as decidedly better able to deal with it, but in the 1980 election, there was a remarkable loss of confidence in the Democratic Party on this issue—only 16 percent picked it. (President Carter had been unable to check the rampant inflation in the late 1970s.) In 1984, things were not much better for the Democrats; only 32 percent saw them as better able to deal with unemployment. In 1988 and 1992, however, the image of the Democratic Party on this issue was almost fully restored to its pre-1980 level, with 50 percent of the "unemployment" Issue Public believing that the Democrats could handle the problem and only around 10 percent favoring the Republicans. After 1992, this favorable image of the Democratic Party faded once again; Republicans began to be seen by about a quarter of the Issue Public as more likely to reduce unemployment.

Then, just as President Bush was finishing his second term, the Great Recession of 2008 hit. In the ANES post-election interview in November 2008, when Bush was still in office, 50 percent cited the economy when asked the MIP question. Unfortunately, in the 2008 survey, the ANES failed to ask which party could best handle problems. We have no way to tell if the Republican Party was now going to be thought of as the party of depression as it was when Hoover was president. There is a major difference, however, in the timing of these events; Hoover was in office for years after the Great Depression began, Bush was there for only three months after the financial crash in 2008. In 2016, unemployment was the top issue and the Republicans had a 2-to-1 advantage on the issue.

The Validity of the Most Important Problems Question

Many social scientists are skeptical about the MIP question. They assume that answers given to this question are simply fleeting comments based on what respondents happen to have heard or come upon recently—probably from the latest news. This view that the MIP question is not measuring issue concerns that the voter already had in mind when interviewed can easily be disproven. In a number of ANES studies, the MIP question was asked in the pre-election interview one or two months *before* the election. If response to this question was only fleeting, how could it still be in mind and have an effect on voting behavior a month or two later? It did have an effect, as we saw in the Introduction (Table 0.1). The weight of the MIP variable was the same whether it was asked in the pre-interview or the post-interview.

Certain political scientists are concerned that the MIP question turns up too many very small segments of the public. Bishop (2005, p. 110–111) complains that "responses are scattered all over the lot." One may wish that the political world where more simple and compact, but it is not. A scattered distribution of issue concerns is to be expected. We have a huge electorate (150 million registered voters), variegated and individualistic. There are at least fifty issues present in any election.[6] The MIP question is a way to measure this reality and to find which of these many issues voters were concerned with. Also, in many elections, the Issue Publics are quite large, ranging from 30 to 70 percent on some issues. From this, the analyst can note which issues were especially important in the election outcome.

Some critics maintain that the second part of the MIP question which asks "Which political party do you think would do a better job in dealing with this problem?" may simply invoke the respondents' party identification, with Republicans almost always picking their party (no matter what the issue) and the Democrats similarly choosing theirs. An examination of the data in the Issue Publics Tables show that this partisan bias has only a minor presence. First, the tables show that there is a very wide variation in the party named as best able to deal with each problem. Party identification is a very stable attitude and certainly would not vary from issue to issue. Note also the large number of issues where neither party is chosen.

Using all ten ANES studies in which the MIP question was asked in its standard form, I examined the relationship between party identification and party chosen as better able to deal with an issue. In seven studies, around 70 percent of *Strong* Republicans did tend to favor their party, but in three elections, 1972, 1976 and 1988, only about 50 percent did. If one looks at *Strong* Democrats, in only three instances, 1964, 1976, and 2000, did around 70 percent choose their party, while in five elections, only about 50 percent named their party as better. In 1980, after Carter's unsuccessful term in office, only 31 percent of *Strong* Democrats felt their party could deal with the problem they mentioned. Thus, even strong party identifiers do not exhibit a consistent tendency to name their own party. Those who have shown party bias most consistently—the Strong Republicans—constitute only about 15 percent of the voters. One must also bear in mind that half of the electorate are weak party identifiers and independents who have little or no partisanship to project into their response to this question.

Notes

1 George Bishop has presented numerous examples of question wording making a major difference in "public opinion" on issues. See his aptly named book "*The Illusion of Public Opinion.*"

2 Real change in positions on the particular issues used in these studies were not likely, that is, having a real attitude at Time 1 and changing one's mind at Time 2. The questions were about issues that had been under discussion for years. Respondents

would have had time to develop an attitude toward the issue, and once arrived at, attitudes usually do not change.

3 These were the causes of the riots as reported in studies such as the McCone Commission report on Watts and The National Advisory Commission on Civil Disorders, known as the Kerner Commission on Detroit and other 1967 riots.

4 The moral decline of the country, first mentioned in 1972, arose, in part, from concern about the youth culture of the late 1960s and early 1970s. "Hippies," "sexual promiscuity," and "Woodstock" were the major referents of those concerned with this issue. Concern for moral decay resumed in 1988 and has continued ever since. Referents for this latter moral concern vary greatly. A few respondents were concerned with abortion and homosexuality. Still more (about 15 percent) specifically mention the absence of God, the Bible, and religion in society. Most respondents who mentioned moral decay were concerned with the breakdown in family life and structure—divorce, single mothers, working mothers. Coupled with this was concern about young people—lack of discipline, promiscuity, teen pregnancy, youth violence, guns, and crime were also mentioned fairly often. A few mentioned the sex and violence on TV and in movies. And about 15 percent saw the problem as one of ethics—lack of honesty, conscience, civility and respect for others, as well as a decline in the sense of community—helping others.

5 President Clinton's feat of balancing the budget was little noticed.

6 Here are some of the many issues present in recent elections: unemployment, inflation, education, regulation of banks, national debt, taxes, global warming, health care, child care, equal pay for women, police treatment of blacks, abortion, gay rights, transgender bathrooms, outsourcing jobs, illegal immigration, crumbling highways and bridges, lack of mass transit and high-speed rail, access to college, veterans benefits, drugs and opioids, poverty, Iraq, Afghanistan, North Korea, ISIS, Syria, domestic terrorist threat, Israel-Palestinian dispute, Iran (nuclear bomb development), military spending, lack of privacy in social media, affordable housing, street gangs, gun control, crowded prisons, future viability of social security, breakdown in families, promiscuousness, campaign finance, stalemated Congress.

Reference

Bishop, George F. 2005. *The Illusion of Public Opinion.* Lanham, MD: Rowman & Littlefield.

4

IMAGES OF THE CANDIDATES

In this chapter, I will briefly present the events and conditions leading up to each campaign, report what the media commentators were saying during the campaign, describe the candidate's conduct and policy positions, and then present the image of the candidate that voters saw—a graphical profile of the candidate based on what respondents said when asked what they like or dislike about a candidate. In the profiles, the horizontal bars are arranged from the most *net* favorable at the top to the least *net* favorable at the bottom. Mention of an item by less than 5 percent of the respondents is not shown in the profiles.

1960: Nixon vs. Kennedy

The main thing that was known about Nixon in 1960 was that he had been President Eisenhower's vice president. Nixon had listless support from Eisenhower. When asked what major contributions Nixon had made to major administrative decisions, Eisenhower replied "give me a week, I might think of one." This was not a promising record to run on.

Kennedy was young (43 years old), Harvard educated, and came from a very wealthy upper-class family. Many commentators thought that he was too young and would not connect with the working-class base of the Democratic Party. He was a war hero who had helped rescue shipmates when their torpedo boat was sunk off the Solomon Islands in World War II. He kept reminding voters of this during the campaign. Late in the campaign, on October 19, Martin Luther King, Jr. was jailed in Atlanta. In a well-publicized gesture, Kennedy reached out to King's wife and arranged bail. (There is no evidence that this gesture made any difference to African-American voters. Kennedy received the same proportion of the African-American vote as Adlai Stevenson had in the 1950s.)

His slogan was a "New Frontier" and he generally supported government action to help people deal with social and economic problems—New Deal type policies such as minimum wage, federal aid to education, medical assistance, and civil rights.

In April 1960, a U2 reconnaissance plane, while flying over the USSR, was shot down. We were caught spying on the USSR and they were very angry. Khrushchev refused to attend a previously scheduled summit conference in Paris until the United States apologized. We refused to apologize, and the conference was never held. Also, in June, a ten-nation disarmament conference failed to reach an agreement on nuclear weapons. Polls showed that more than half of the American people thought war with the USSR was inevitable. With the Cold War heating up, Kennedy devoted much of his campaign to showing that he would be a strong leader against the USSR.

In 1959, Castro's revolution in Cuba succeeded. Kennedy never failed to mention that communism was now just 90 miles from our shores in Cuba ("Cuber" as he pronounced it.)

And then there was the Catholic issue. Al Smith, a Catholic Democrat, ran for president in 1928 and was soundly defeated (receiving only 41 percent of the vote). Now another Catholic, Kennedy, was seeking nomination. In 1960, candidates were still being nominated at conventions controlled by party leaders. There were some primaries, such as one in West Virginia, but the nominating system had not yet shifted to all-primaries. Party leaders were highly skeptical of Kennedy's ability to overcome anti-Catholic bias. In order to show them that times had changed since 1928 and that bias against Catholics had subsided, Kennedy decided to use the West Virginia primary as a test case. West Virginia was predominately Protestant yet Kennedy won the primary and was subsequently nominated at the Democratic convention.

But concern about a Catholic in the White House kept emerging during the campaign, so Kennedy decided to confront the issue head-on. He gave a speech before the Greater Houston Ministerial Association on September 12, 1960. He emphasized that he believed in the absolute separation of church and state, was against federal aid to parochial schools, and would make decisions without regard to outside religious pressures. This tended to dampen down the Catholic issue, in public commentary at least. (What people were thinking in private was another matter.)

A major feature of the 1960 campaign were the debates between Nixon and Kennedy. Television had just arrived in most living rooms and the debates were the first time this new medium was used in a presidential campaign. The first debate drew a large audience. Estimates of public reaction indicated that Kennedy had done a bit better. He was relaxed, sharp, knowledgeable, and he looked directly at the camera, making viewers feel he was talking to them. In the first debate, Nixon looked haggard, pale, and had perspiration on his face. (Those who heard the debate on the radio, without seeing Nixon, thought he had done better than Kennedy.)

What Was on Voters' Minds—the Profiles

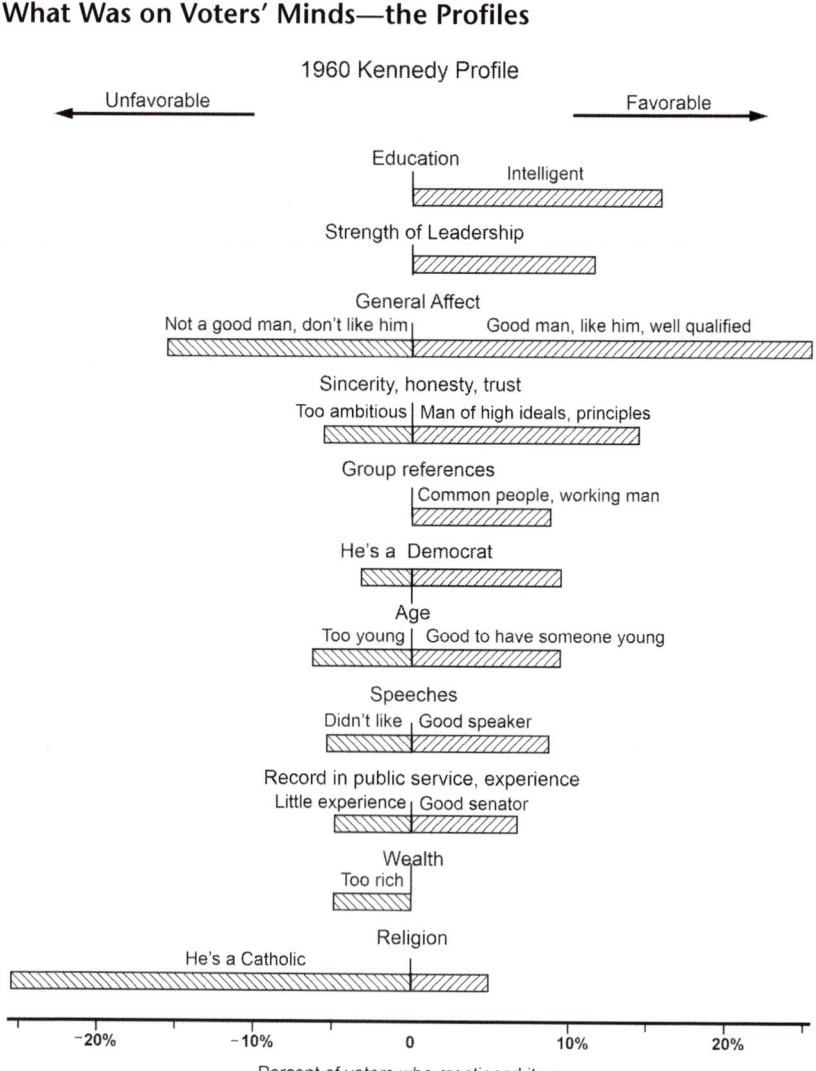

1960 Kennedy Profile

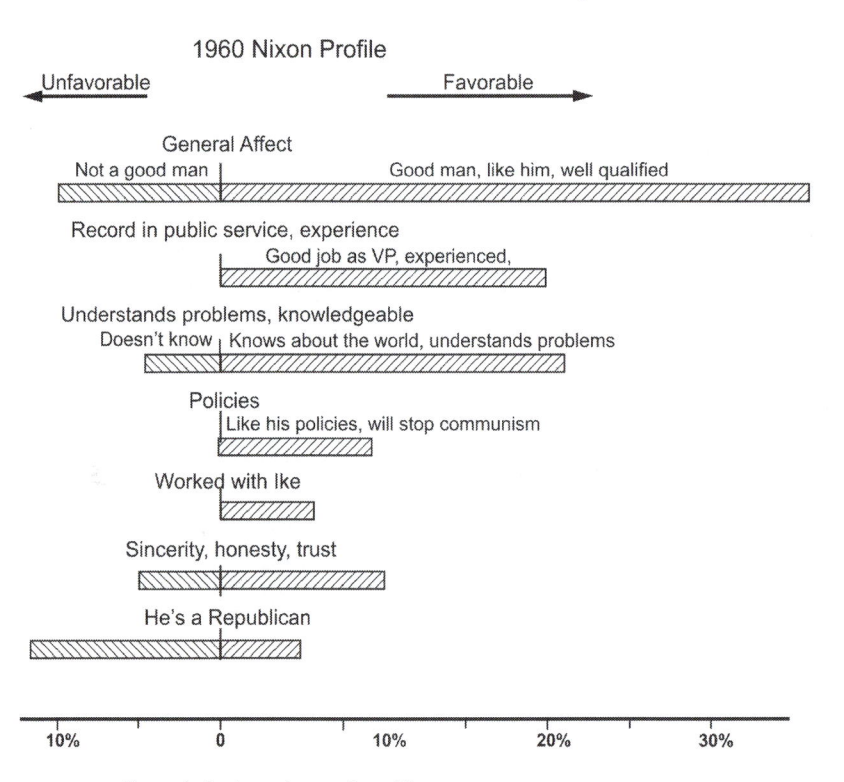

1960 Nixon Profile

Percent of voters who mentioned item

Looking at Kennedy's profile, we notice, first of all, that a large segment of the public had a negative attitude toward Kennedy because he was Catholic. They were concerned that the Pope would have a major influence on Kennedy and his policies. A few even went so far as to think the Pope might move into the White House. Apparently, Kennedy's talk at the Houston ministers conference had not quieted anti-Catholic fears. Twenty-seven percent of Protestant Democrats deserted their party and voted for Nixon.

Kennedy did have some things going for him. He was generally well-liked, was seen as educated and intelligent, and as someone who could be trusted. (It turns out that his Harvard education was an asset.) He was also seen as a leader, perhaps because of his PT boat experience. He was also helped by being a Democrat and championing the working man. His age was, on net, an asset but there were a number of negative remarks about his wealth (too rich).

Nixon

Looking at Nixon's profile, we see that he was very well liked and thought to be knowledgeable about the world. He was specifically praised for his good job as VP and having worked with Eisenhower.

When respondents were asked about problems facing the country in 1960, we saw in Chapter 3 that 70 percent mentioned either the Cold War, the need for defense spending, or the need to negotiate with the USSR. Yet despite the U-2 incident and Cuba going communist when a Republican was in the White House, about 40 percent of voters thought that Republicans would do better in handling Cold War problems compared with about 25 percent for Democrats.

Thus, even though many commentators thought Nixon would be hurt by lack of support from Eisenhower, that he did poorly in the debates, and was Vice President in an administration that was doing poorly in foreign relations, Nixon was very popular—61 percent of the comments about him were positive.

What did hurt him a bit was being a Republican in a time of Democratic ascendency. Kennedy won because he had a head-start—the normal vote at that time was 54 percent Democratic. But he won by the thinnest of margins—100,000 votes. Being a Catholic hurt him badly.

1964: Johnson vs. Goldwater

Barry Goldwater was a true conservative and a true Republican. He had written a book titled *The Conscience of a Conservative* and was received with great enthusiasm at the Republican Convention that nominated him. He proudly proclaimed that "Extremism in defense of liberty is no vice, moderation in pursuit of justice is no virtue." He was indeed extreme. While campaigning in the New Hampshire primary, he said that Social Security should be made voluntary. He did not repeat that again, but the damage had already been done—it had swept the country by word of mouth. Goldwater was fervently for freedom and against government activity.

His foreign policy was particularly belligerent. He wanted to give Army commanders in Europe the option of using tactical atomic weapons without permission from Washington. He proposed using low-yield atomic bombs to defoliate Vietnam. His speeches were full of comments about nuclear warfare with words like "push the button" and "brinkmanship."

During the campaign season in June 1964, the Senate passed a Civil Rights bill. Senator Goldwater voted against it. Thus, he demonstrated clearly that he was not for civil rights and desegregation. He won five states in the Deep South—South Carolina, Georgia, Alabama, Mississippi, and Louisiana—but lost every other state except his home state of Arizona.

Johnson

Lyndon Johnson, who had become president when Kennedy was assassinated, had been president for less than a year when the 1964 presidential election campaign began. He had already accomplished a great deal. He used the political skills that he had learned as Majority Leader in the Senate plus the power of the presidency to get two major pieces of legislation through Congress—the Civil Rights Act of 1964 and an anti-poverty bill. In the campaign, he stressed two things: that he would be loyal to the Kennedy agenda and that he would work toward developing a "Great Society" that would end poverty and assure full employment.

The war in Vietnam was heating up. Early in the campaign, Johnson promised not to send American boys to fight in Vietnam, saying "we are not about to send American boys 10,000 miles away from home to do what Asian boys ought to be doing themselves." But then, two incidents in Vietnamese waters (the Tonkin Gulf) were reported. An American destroyer, on a clandestine intelligence mission, reportedly was attacked by small Vietnamese torpedo boats. Johnson went to Congress on August 7, 1964, and got a resolution that said he could "take all necessary measures to repel any armed attack against forces of the United States and to prevent aggression." We already had over 10,000 military in Vietnam in an advisory capacity. Johnson sent more "advisors" and started bombing North Vietnam. And then in March 1965, two months after his inauguration, Johnson broke his campaign promise and began sending ground troops.

On September 7, 1964, the now famous "Daisy girl" ad appeared on TV. It showed a little girl in a field of daisies happily picking the petals of a daisy, one at a time. She counted them as she went. But when she got near 10, a male voice is heard saying "10," "9," "8," and when he gets to "0," a mushroom-shaped cloud is seen on the horizon. This was obviously intended to play into the fears that Goldwater might use nuclear weapons. The Johnson campaign pulled the ad after only this one showing. But many voters saw it because the media replayed it again and again.

(This was the beginning of two very unfortunate aspects of election campaigns. It was the first major attack ad and it changed the role of the media from reporting to participating. From then on, TV "news" has included partisan propaganda—the showing of partisan campaign ads.)

What Was on Voters' Minds—the Profiles

Looking at Goldwater's profile, we see a candidate who was considered a fanatic and a warmonger. He was not well liked and his general policy stances were rejected. Being a conservative was not an asset and his vote against the Civil Rights Act earned him many negative comments. About the only things he had going for him were that he was seen as honest and sincere and that he was for states' rights, balanced budgets and cutting government activity. But an equal number of voters disliked other policies such as changing Social Security and not supporting Medicare.

Johnson was praised for almost everything. He was very well liked and was seen as an experienced, good leader who was continuing Kennedy's polices.

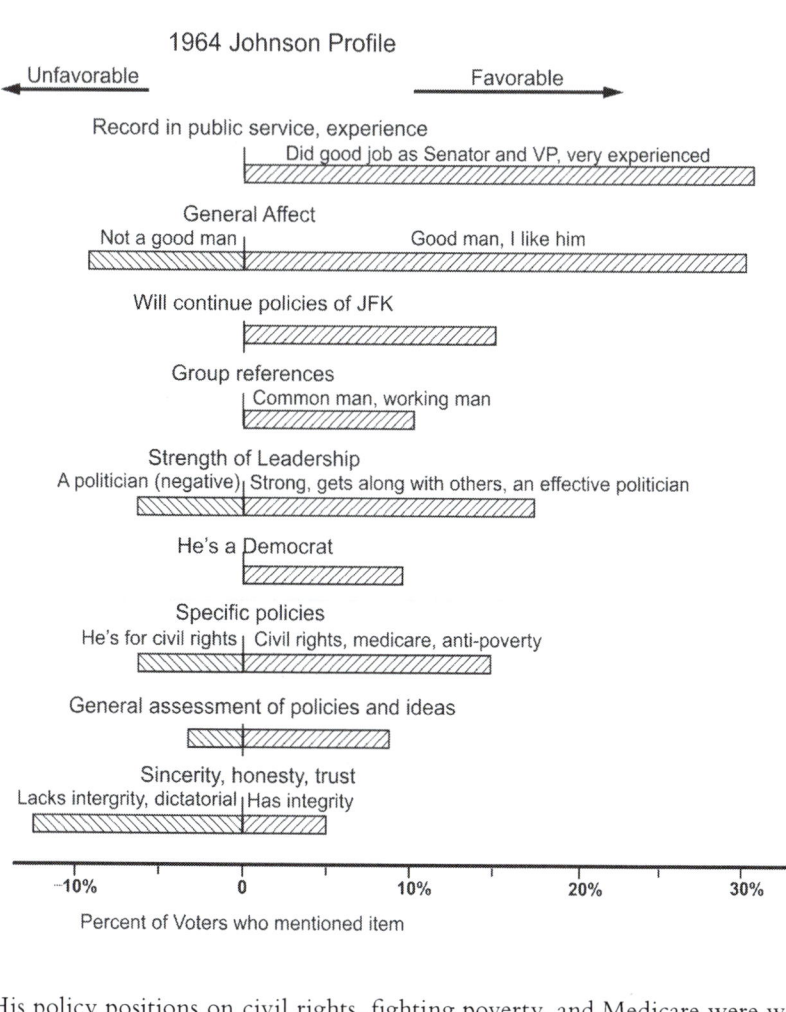

1964 Johnson Profile

His policy positions on civil rights, fighting poverty, and Medicare were well received. If we look at the Issue Publics (Chapter 3) we see that Johnson was addressing the major issue concerns of the electorate—civil rights, problems of the aged, and the Cold War.

Although we were not heavily involved yet, there was an Issue Public concerned with Vietnam in 1964. Despite Goldwater, Republicans were thought somewhat better able to handle it (Issue Publics Table in Chapter 3). Looking at Johnson's profile, we see no mention of Vietnam. This was perhaps because he had promised not to send troops and the implications of the Tonkin Bay resolution were not yet known.

In all, Johnson was seen very favorably (63 percent of comments were positive) and Goldwater was seen very unfavorably (64 percent of comments were negative). The strong dislike of Goldwater was a major plus for Johnson; thus, a monumental landslide victory for LBJ.

1964 Goldwater Profile

← Unfavorable   Favorable →

Sincerity, honesty

Specific policies

Would change social security,   States rights, balance budgets,
he's against medicare   would cut government actiivity

He's a conservative

Civil rights

Fanatic, extremist

General assessment of policies and ideas

Warlike
Poor control of nuclear weapons

Strength of Leadership
Impulsive

General Affect
Not a good man, don't like him   Good man

Speeches

-20%   -10%   0   10%

Percent of Voters who mentioned item

1972: Nixon vs. McGovern

As the 1972 election approached, there were two major problems looming—the highly unpopular war in Vietnam was still going on and there was high inflation. Nixon was determined to be reelected and did everything in his power to bring that about. First, he removed the inflation problem by freezing prices and wages. Here was a Republican president massively interfering with the market-based economy. No wonder this freeze was called "the Shock." And

Nixon began to eliminate the Vietnam issue by starting to withdraw troops and by sending Secretary of State Kissinger to Paris to meet with North Vietnam leaders to work out a peace treaty. Nixon also went to China in February 1972, a move many saw as a positive step in international relations.

Furthermore, Nixon formed a campaign organization called Campaign to Reelect the President (CREEP). That organization engaged in dirty tricks such as planting a fake letter in a major New Hampshire newspaper, which implied that the leading Democratic candidate, Edmund Muskie, was prejudiced against French-Canadians. (Many French-Canadians had emigrated to New Hampshire.) Muskie teared up while giving a speech to deny the accusation. This made him look unable to absorb criticism and maintain emotional stability. As a result of that letter, Muskie did very poorly in the New Hampshire primary and he never recovered in later primaries. CREEP had gotten rid of the strongest Democratic candidate.

On June 17, 1972, during the general election campaign, CREEP broke into the Democratic Party headquarters in the Watergate hotel and stole documents. There was little media coverage during the campaign and no mention of it in voters' comments about Nixon. (It was not until after Nixon was elected that Watergate began to be investigated.)

McGovern

George McGovern won enough primaries to become the Democratic Party nominee. His main platform plank was to get out of Vietnam. He also brought up other issues such as giving amnesty to those who had fled to Canada to avoid the draft, favored choice on the abortion issue, and proposed legalizing marijuana. The media summed up these three issues by calling them the "three A's"—Amnesty, Abortion, and Acid (drugs). Media commentators thought these issues were too liberal and would hurt him. McGovern also suggested helping the poor with a government subsidy.[1]

With his major issue (Vietnam) taken away by the troop withdrawals and the Kissinger negotiations, McGovern was not doing well in the polls. Democratic Party leaders were very concerned that he was too liberal. They enlisted Humphrey to get out on the campaign trail and try to defeat McGovern in the primaries. Humphrey's attacks on McGovern added to McGovern's negatives.

The Democratic convention was disorganized and contentious, which resulted in McGovern having to give his acceptance speech in the wee hours of the morning; it made McGovern look like he was unable to lead an organization. And then there was the Eagleton affair. McGovern had chosen Thomas Eagleton to be his running mate. It was soon discovered that Eagleton had had psychological problems earlier in life, but McGovern said he would back him "1000 percent." A few days later, he dumped him.

What Was on Voters' Minds—the Profiles

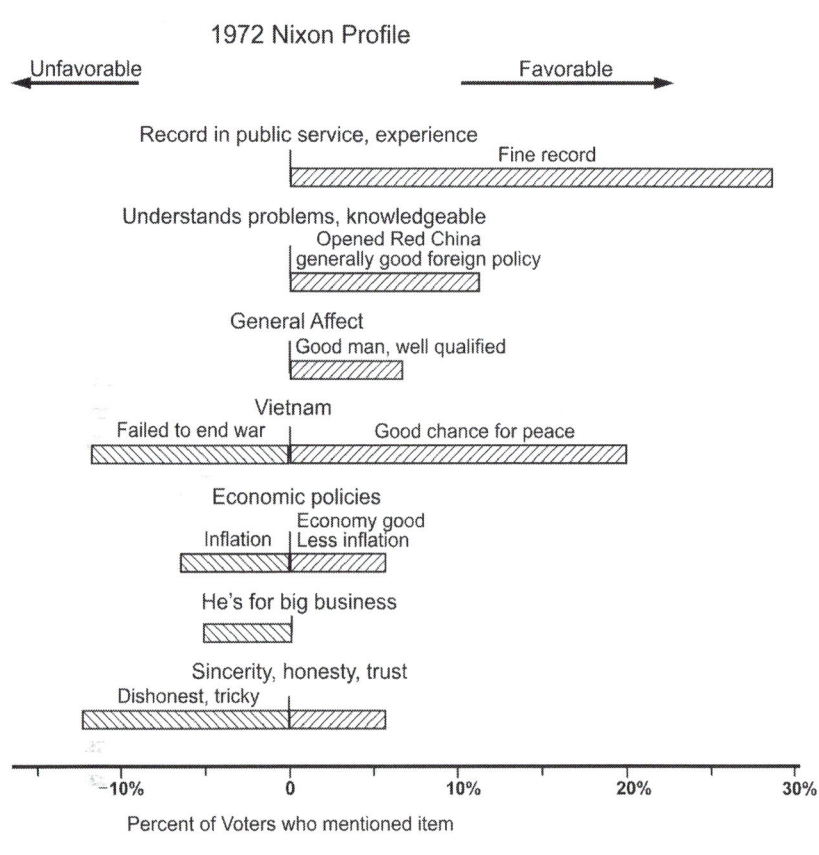

1972 Nixon Profile

Unfavorable ← → Favorable

Record in public service, experience
Fine record

Understands problems, knowledgeable
Opened Red China
generally good foreign policy

General Affect
Good man, well qualified

Vietnam
Failed to end war Good chance for peace

Economic policies
Economy good
Inflation | Less inflation

He's for big business

Sincerity, honesty, trust
Dishonest, tricky

-10% 0 10% 20% 30%

Percent of Voters who mentioned item

First of all, Nixon's profile shows that many voters thought that he was the candidate who could bring peace in Vietnam and McGovern netted nothing on the Vietnam issue—just as many thought McGovern could not bring peace as thought he could. The ploy of sending Kissinger to Paris to start peace talks had worked. We see in Nixon's profile that he had also succeeded in negating the inflation issue by freezing wages and prices. Only a very few faulted Nixon on inflation and that was countered by an equal number who liked his economic policies.

On the other hand, Nixon was often referred to as "tricky Dick" and we see in his profile that many voters believed that this was an appropriate moniker.

A few—a very few—disliked McGovern because he was a liberal and there was no mention of the "Three A's" issues. The overwhelming problem for McGovern was that he was a very poor leader—weak and indecisive. Many explicitly mentioned the Eagleton affair.

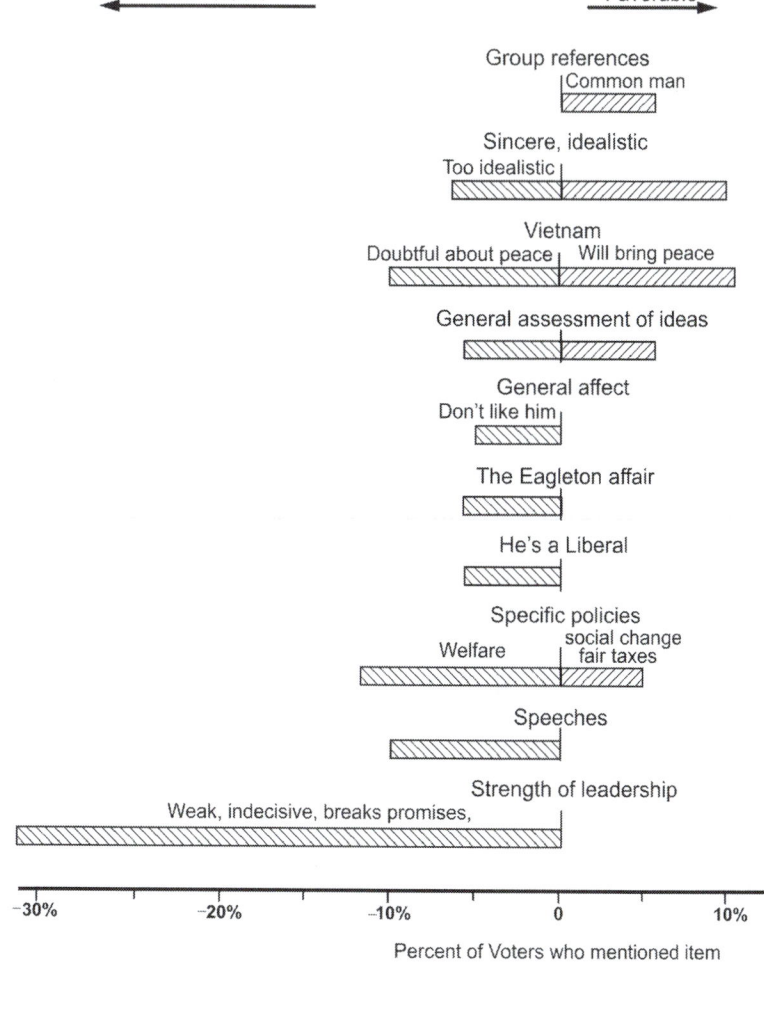

1972 McGovern Profile

In short, McGovern lost because he was up against CREEP and an incumbent president who preempted his major issue (Vietnam) and was willing to interfere with the economy in order to win. McGovern's weakness as a leader and his indecisiveness also hurt him very badly.

1976: Ford vs. Carter

President Nixon resigned on August 9, 1974 in order to keep from being impeached. For over a year, the nation had watched as a special congressional committee, headed by Senator Sam Ervin, revealed evidence of Nixon's involvement in the Watergate burglary and his attempt to cover it up. It was a long, painful spectacle for the American people. On the day Nixon left, Vice President Gerald Ford was sworn in as President and gave a brief speech to the American people saying "my fellow Americans, our long national nightmare is over." To assure it was over, a month later Ford pardoned Nixon for any crime he may have committed or participated in while in office. Without that pardon, Nixon might have gone on trial and the nightmare would have continued. Ford's job approval ratings plummeted—apparently most Americans thought Nixon should be tried and punished. But some in the public thought he had done the right thing and that view had a major impact on their vote (as we will see in Chapter 5).

Ford was a mild-mannered, unassuming, straightforward, but ineffectual person. For example, his answer to the serious problem of inflation was to hand out "WIN" ("Whip Inflation Now") buttons. In one of the debates, he implied that he did not know that Eastern Europe was communist (a gaffe that the media loved to keep pointing out).

Carter

Carter was unknown before running for president. His family owned a peanut farm in Georgia, he had been a Navy officer, and he had served one term as governor of Georgia (but that was his only political experience). He was a very religious man who epitomized Christian values and taught Sunday school.

When he ran for governor, his political advisor was Hamilton Jordan and he chose Jordan to be his campaign manager in his run for the presidency. Jordan had figured out how to win in the primary system. First of all, you win the first two primaries (Iowa and New Hampshire). This gets you noticed. Carter sent campaign workers North to help with that effort and he won those two states. Then, he worked tirelessly, holding 1,500 town meetings in every state. He was relaxed and informal and related to people. He started the campaign by promising "never to tell a lie." People trusted him and he was totally divorced from scandal-ridden Washington.

In the general election campaign, one of the most noteworthy events was Carter agreeing to be interviewed by *Playboy* magazine (famous for its nude centerfolds). His desire to be open and honest resulted in him admitting that he had "looked upon a lot of women with lust" and "I've committed adultery in my heart many times." This shocking revelation swept the country. In addition, Carter was not very forthcoming on his positions on many issues. He was vague and uncertain.

What Was on Voters' Minds—the Profiles

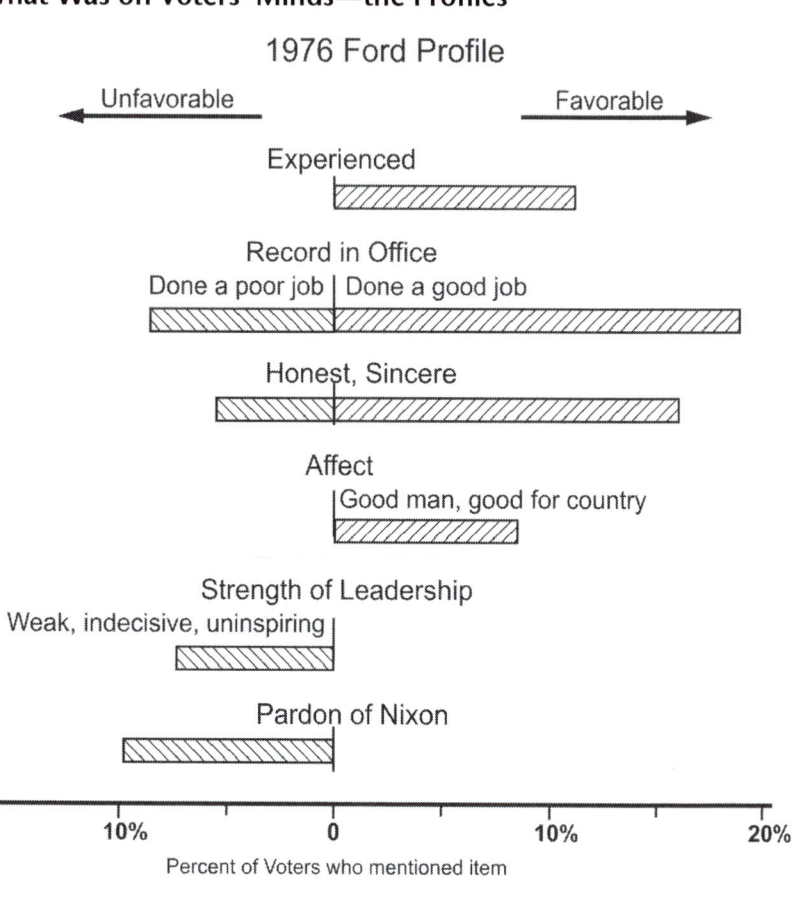

1976 Ford Profile

First of all, the two things that had attracted a lot of media commentary, Ford's Eastern Europe gaffe and Carter's *Playboy* interview drew almost no comments when voters were asked their likes and dislikes of the candidates. Ford was seen as experienced with a good record in office, as honest and sincere, and as good for the country. Some did find him weak and uninspiring, and 10 percent did not like the pardon. Carter was seen as honest, a good religious and moral man, and as supporting the working man. His negatives were that he was inexperienced, weak and indecisive, and too vague on issues.

The results of the election were extremely close, with Carter winning by a very slim margin. Why the election was so close will be explained Chapter 5.

1976 Carter Profile

Unfavorable ← → Favorable

Honest, sincere

Affect
Good man, will be good president

Group references
for the common man, working people

Religious, moral

Inexperienced

Vague, doesn't mean what he says

Weak, indecisive

10%   0   10%   20%
Percent of Voters who mentioned item

1980: Carter vs. Reagan

As the 1980 election approached, President Carter was in deep trouble. There was a runaway inflation with prices going up by as much as 14 percent a year. (Inflation had been 7 percent when Carter took office.) Prices were going up so fast that supermarkets had to quit trying to use price labels on shelf edges—they could not keep up with the rapid changes. Home prices were skyrocketing and mortgage costs were rising rapidly. A great many women who wanted to be stay-at-home moms could no longer do so, as their income was necessary to pay the mortgage and put groceries on the table.[2]

At the same time, the economy was not growing—we had what was called "stagflation." Carter was very concerned and gave an address to the nation in which he said we had a "crisis of confidence," which was a crisis that strikes at the very heart and spirit of our national will. We can see this crisis in the growing doubt about the meaning of our own lives and in the loss of a unity of purpose for our nation.

This was known as the "malaise" speech.

Then in 1979, there was a revolution in Iran that overthrew the Shaw, a longtime ally of the United States. In November, as part of the revolution, students stormed our embassy and took sixty-six Americans hostage. For over a year, the American media gave the public daily reminders that our hostages were still there. Carter seemed helpless. He did try to send helicopters with special forces to rescue them, but several helicopters had mechanical problems and the mission had to be aborted. Carter never tried again.

Carter did have one major accomplishment during his tenure in office; he acted as an intermediary between the Egyptian president and the Israeli prime minister and got them to agree to a peace treaty. But the situation in Israel has almost never been mentioned by American voters in any election, and this was no exception. Only 1.5 percent mentioned this peace treaty in the 1980 interviews.

Three important and highly visible positions in Carter's administration were Chief of Staff, Hamilton Jordan; Press Secretary, Jody Powell; and Director of the Office of Management and Budget (OMB), Burt Lance. Jordan had engineered Carter's nomination in the 1976 primaries, and all three were with him during the 1976 campaign. Before joining the Carter team, Lance had been Chairman of the Board of Calhoun First National Bank of Georgia. After he became Director of OMB, questions were raised by the press and Congress about corruption at the Bank while Lance was Chairman of the Board. These accusations of wrongdoing forced Lance to resign as Director of OMB. Jordan received bad press (usually false rumors), but there was one fairly serious charge that he had snorted cocaine during a visit to a New York night club. In 1979, a special counsel was appointed to investigate the accusation. The investigation resulted in no charges, but Jordan's reputation had been besmirched.

Reagan

Ronald Reagan was an actor who was known for his many roles in the movies. He was sometimes called "The Gipper" for a role he once played. He had also been elected governor of California in 1966. He was 69 years old when he ran for president in 1980 and became the oldest president ever elected. He was very conservative, concentrating on lowering taxes and strengthening the military. Otherwise, he was little known and voters' image of him was rather shallow.

What Was on Voters' Minds—the Profiles

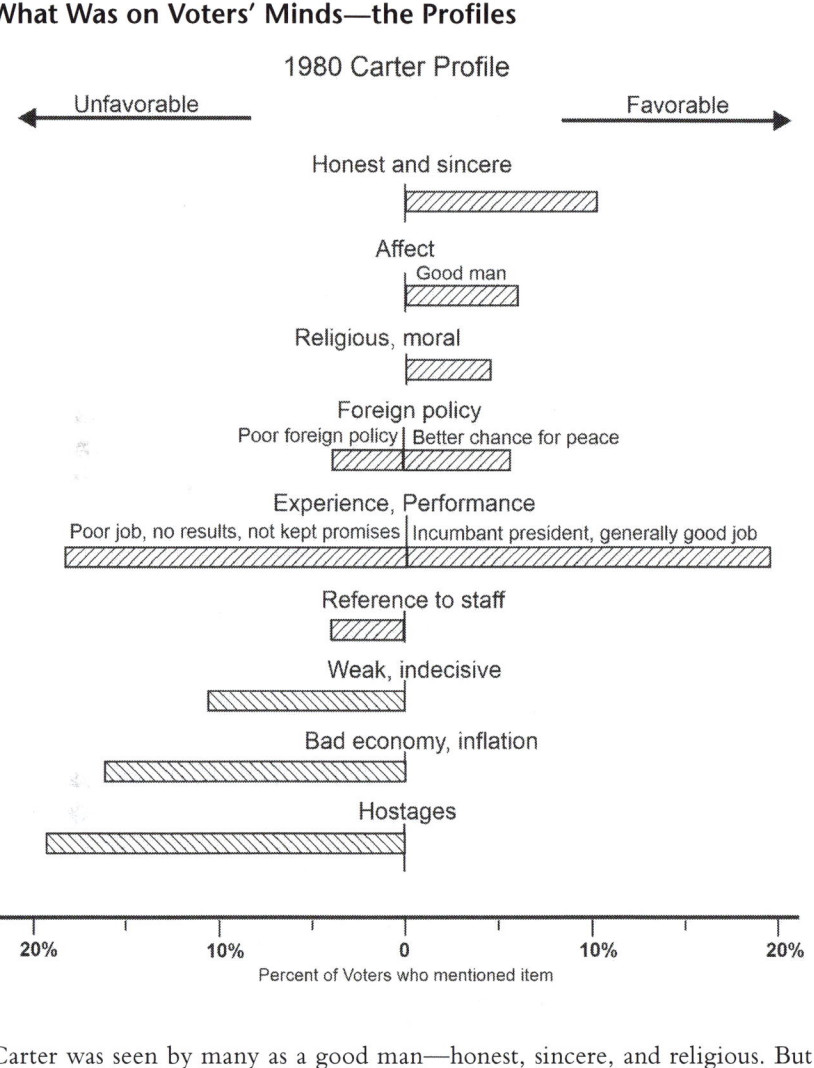

1980 Carter Profile

Percent of Voters who mentioned item

Carter was seen by many as a good man—honest, sincere, and religious. But many more saw him as weak and indecisive. His inability to deal with a runaway inflation and the hostage crisis were very often cited as reasons to dislike him. Twenty percent saw him as having generally been a good president, but an equal number saw him as being a poor president, not accomplishing anything, and not living up to his promises. The Burt Lance and Hamilton Jordan scandals also hurt him a bit (see "Reference to staff" in the negative comment column). Overall, Carter had a very negative image.

As evidence of voters' unfamiliarity with Reagan, the comments about him were scattered with many different things mentioned, each by less than 5 percent. The only things that stood out were that 12 percent liked him

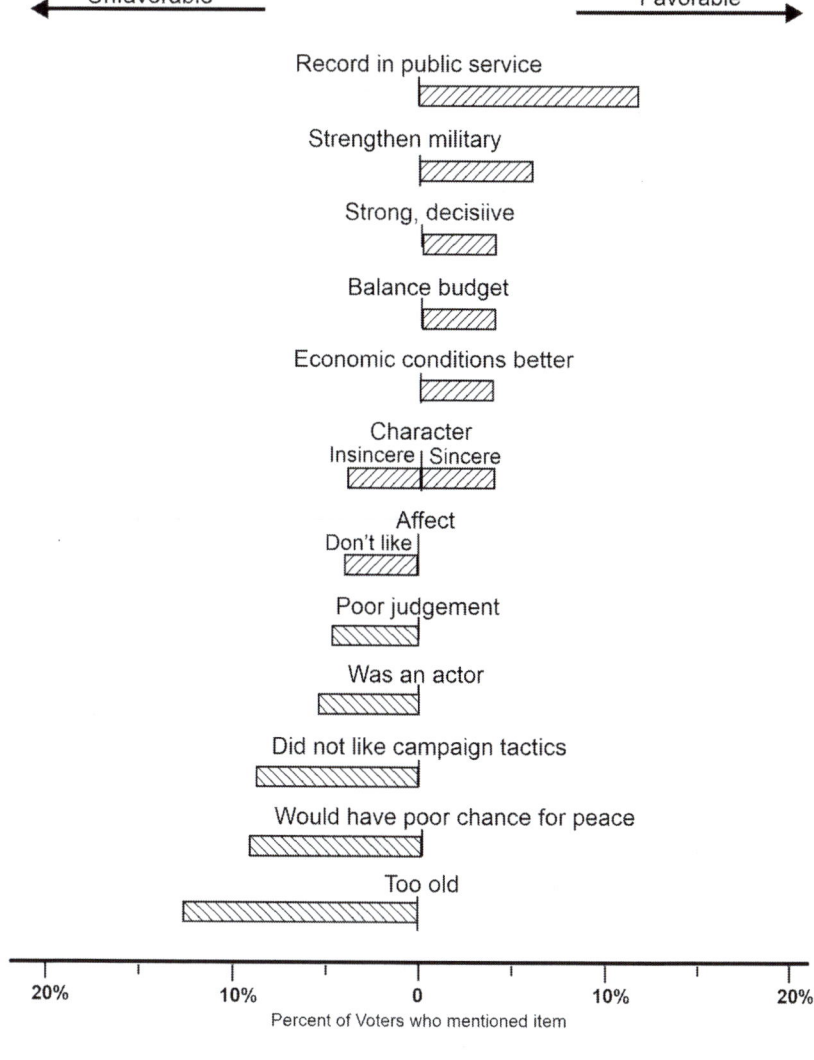

1980 Reagan Profile

◄───── Unfavorable ━━━━━━   Favorable ─────►

Record in public service

Strengthen military

Strong, decisiive

Balance budget

Economic conditions better

Character
Insincere | Sincere

Affect
Don't like |

Poor judgement

Was an actor

Did not like campaign tactics

Would have poor chance for peace

Too old

20%   10%   0   10%   20%
Percent of Voters who mentioned item

because of this record of public service (presumably because he had been governor of California). Dislike of his campaign tactics and the feeling he would not promote peace drew the comments of 8 percent each. The main concern of voters was his age, mentioned by 13 percent. Interestingly, his career as an actor did not detract much. Only 5 percent mentioned it negatively; many more thought that he had the experience and qualities to be president. Some of the qualities that were mentioned favorably were that he would be a strong, decisive leader, balance the budget, and improve economic conditions.

1984: Reagan vs. Mondale

During his first term in office, Ronald Reagan proved to be the conservative that Republicans had always wished for. He strongly believed in a free market economy and less government ("gov'ment" as he pronounced it). He also believed in a strong military. However, he did not go after established government programs such as Social Security and Medicare. Indeed, he rescued Social Security from potential bankruptcy by setting up a bipartisan commission in 1983 that made recommendations to shore-up the program. However, early in Reagan's term he did lower some Social Security benefits and severely restricted eligibility for disability. It is noteworthy that Reagan presided over the passage of an immigration reform bill that included amnesty.

One of the first things he did was to enact a large tax cut—the largest in history. The top rate was dropped from 70 percent to 50 percent and the bottom rate was lowered from 14 percent to 11 percent. The capital gains tax was reduced from 28 percent to 20 percent. At the same time, Reagan began a massive build-up of the military. Plans were drawn up to deploy the MX intercontinental missile and the controversial anti-missile program, the Strategic Defense Initiative (SDI), was undertaken. Also, the production of a neutron bomb was begun.

A large increase in spending on the military and a large decrease in revenue was a recipe for sizable budget deficits. Reagan, however, believed in a theory developed by an economist, Laffer, that tax cuts would stimulate investment and spending to a point where lost tax revenue would be replenished by booming businesses and employment. The theory did not work and the national debt skyrocketed. As we saw in the Issues Table in Chapter 3, the debt was one of the two top issue concerns in 1984. The other issue of concern was the arms race and threat of a nuclear war with the USSR.

Almost as soon as Reagan took office in 1981, the double-digit inflation went down to normal levels. One of the theories that explain this is that, all during the 1970s, businesses were afraid to be caught with their prices down as they had been when Nixon froze prices in 1972, so they kept raising prices during the presidency of Carter to keep ahead of a possible freeze. If Nixon, a Republican, had frozen prices, what might Carter, the Democrat, do? When Reagan was elected, there was now a true conservative in the White House who could be trusted not to interfere with the economy. The fear of a sudden freeze was over; there was no longer a need to raise prices in anticipation of it.

In August 1981, the air traffic controllers went on strike. Reagan refused to honor their picket lines and he hired replacements. Unions, generally, were weakened by this example of strike breaking.

In the first debate of the 1984 campaign, Reagan seemed to be lost at times, stumbling and forgetting what he wanted to say. Commentators began asking if he was too old. (He was 73.) However, he was sharp in the second debate so the age issue subsided. But, as we will see in Reagan's profile, it did not go away.

Starting with a speech he gave as the 1980 election campaign began and repeated often throughout his presidency, Reagan spoke of hope and America being a "shining city on a hill." His campaign also featured the famous "Morning in America" ad narrated by Reagan himself.

What Voters Thought about Reagan—His Profile

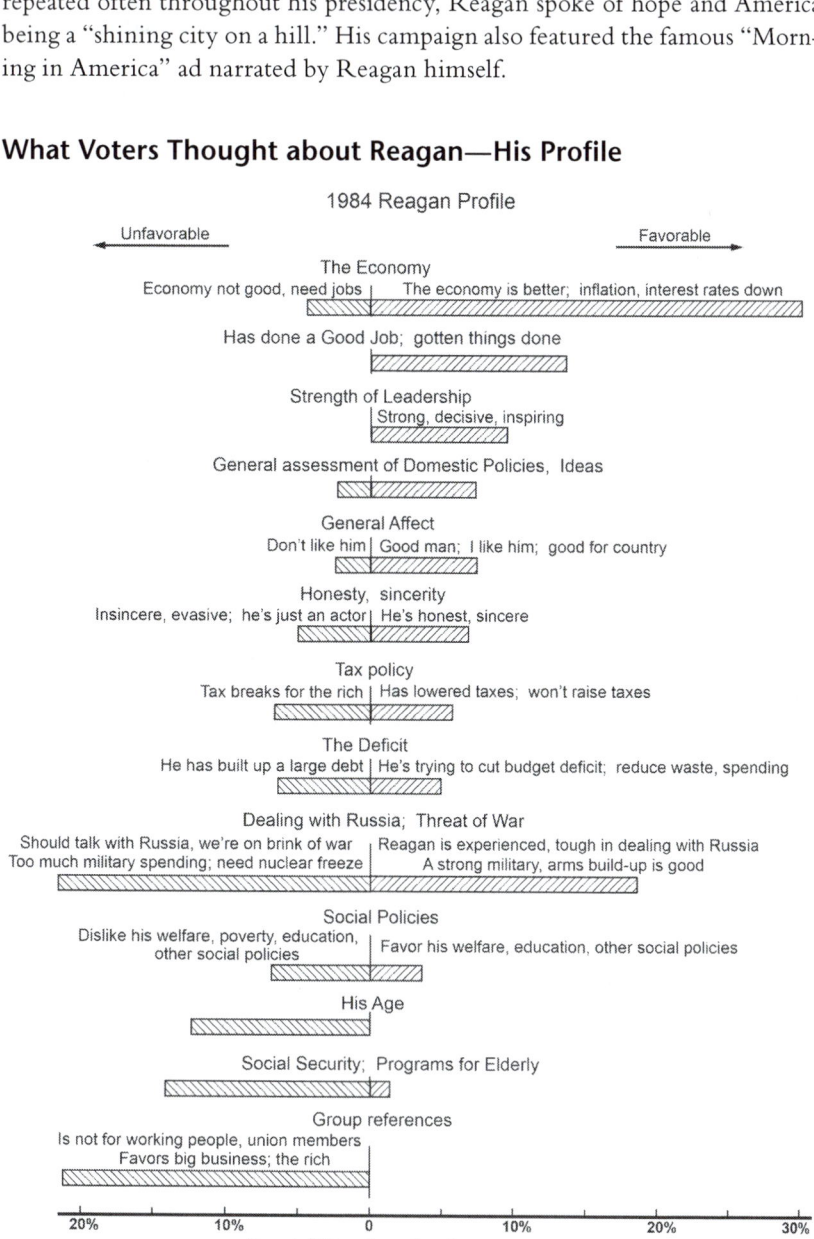

1984 Reagan Profile

Reagan was given a lot of credit for ending inflation. His increase in military strength got mixed reviews with many approving the arms buildup and his tough stand in dealing with the USSR, while an equal number were alarmed that we were on the brink of war and thought too much was being spent on the military. The massive tax cuts received little comment, with as many against them as for them.

There were not a lot of comments about his role in the deficit and they were mixed—both positive and negative. When we look at the Issue Tables in Chapter 3, we note that the Republican Party was seen by many (39 percent) as the party better able to deal with the deficit problem. (Only 21 percent saw the Democrats as able to deal with it.) Thus, despite the fact that the deficit was a result of Reagan's policies, the Republican Party was none-the-less seen as the cure. Perhaps this was because the Republican Party has traditionally been noted for its fiscal responsibility.

His stance on government activity did not receive enough comments to be included in his profile and his positions on social programs were mostly negative. Interestingly, he was not identified as a conservative; the word "conservative" was almost never used by respondents.

Most negative comments had to do with Reagan's lack of support for working people, union members, and the poor, while he was seen as a friend of big business and the rich. His age was a major negative. Recall that, early in his administration, he very publicly lowered some Social Security benefits and restricted eligibility for disability. "Social Security" was a major negative in Reagan's profile.

Overall, there were almost as many negative attitudes as positive. *Reagan was not popular.* Yet Reagan won in a massive landslide; the only state Mondale won was his home state of Minnesota. The reason for this win will be explained in Chapter 5.

Mondale

Walter Mondale started his campaign with two strikes against him: He had been vice president in the troubled Carter administration and he was a dull, uninspiring speaker who was up against "the great communicator." Also, in the primaries, his major rivals, John Glenn and Gary Hart, attacked him, saying he was the candidate of big labor and "special interests," and was "making promises to everyone."

Mondale was bold enough to choose a woman, Geraldine Ferraro, as a running mate—the first time a woman had been nominated for such a high office. He was also responsible enough to tackle the deficit problem by saying it could not be solved without raising taxes.

What Voters Thought about Mondale—His Profile

1984 Mondale Profile

Unfavorable ◄─────────────   ─────────────► Favorable

Group references
For working people, unions, the poor, minorities

Peace, nuclear war; dealing with Russia

"He's a Democrat"

Honesty, sincerity

Experience, capability
Not capable
No confidence in him | Experienced, conscientious

Choice of VP running mate (Ferraro)

Defense Policy
Need strong military | Will reduce defense spending

General Affect
Don't like him; not a good man | Good man; I like him

Tax policy

Not his own man
Will do anything to please others
Controlled by unions, other special interests

The Campaign
Too negative
Promises anything to win | Like what he says

Record in Office; Connection to Carter

Strength of Leadership
Weak, wishy-washy, uninspiring

| −20% | −10% | 0 | 10% | 20% |

Percent of Voters who mentioned item

Looking at Mondale's profile, we see that he was favored for being a Democrat and supporting working people, and the poor—groups that have traditionally been supported by Democratic candidates. He was also quite strongly supported by those who wanted détente with USSR and were concerned with a nuclear war. His choice of Geraldine Ferraro as the running mate drew a lot of attention, half favorable and half unfavorable. The two most mentioned negatives were uninspiring leadership and the fact that he had been Carter's VP. A third major criticism was that he ran a negative campaign. The fourth largest criticism was his being supported by special interests and was promising anything to win—the Glenn and Hart accusations stuck. His tax policy was not the first or second most mentioned negative, but the fifth. About 11 percent dislike it, but 5 percent praised him for it—a net negative of 6 percent. *Thus, his call for a tax increase to help balance the budget was not a major factor in his defeat.*

1988: H. W. Bush vs. Dukakis

When he ran for president in 1988, George Herbert Walker Bush had had a wealth of experience in government service. He was a congressman from 1967 to 1971, Ambassador to the UN (1971–1973), Chief of the Liaison Office in China (1974–1975), and Director of the CIA (1976–1977). He then served for eight years as Ronald Reagan's vice president.

Being Reagan's vice president was not an asset since the last two years of Reagan's second term were mired in the Iran–Contra scandal. Reagan wanted to give aid to the anti-communist insurgents (the Contras) in Nicaragua, but Congress passed the Boland amendment, which restricted activities of the CIA and the Defense Department in providing such aid. In the meantime, in the Middle East, war had broken out between Iraq and Iran. We sided with Iraq. Iranian-backed terrorists took seven American diplomats and private contractors hostage in Lebanon. Iran was willing to help free them if we supplied them with arms. Reagan agreed to supply those arms and the hostages were released. It was later discovered that half of the money for Iranian arms was missing. An investigation showed that the money had been diverted to the Contras in Nicaraguan. Reagan's approval rating dropped precipitously by 16 percentage points. A commission, led by Senator John Tower, was established to investigate this blatant end-run around Congress. The public was continually reminded of the scandal for the remainder of Reagan's term. Vice President Bush claimed not to have been involved, but as we shall see in his profile, many in the public did not believe him.

Bush hired Lee Atwater to be his campaign manager. Atwater was known for his Machiavellian style and he advised Bush to kept Dukakis off-balance with constant attacks. The Bush campaign made sure that voters knew about Dukakis' anti-death penalty and pro-choice positions. In the debates, Bush kept saying that Dukakis was a "card carrying member of the ACLU" and Bush would turn toward Dukakis and sneeringly say that he was a "liberal" as if it was something bad. Dukakis stood silent and never explained or defended his liberal beliefs.

Bush chose Dan Quayle, an unknown Senator, as his running mate. Many thought Quayle had too little experience, was a very poor speaker, and often seemed rattled and uncertain.

Dukakis

Dukakis was serving his second term as governor of Massachusetts when he decided to run in the 1988 presidential primaries. (He had previously served as governor from 1975 to 1979.) He got a very good head-start by achieving an impressive win in the first primary—New Hampshire. This was no doubt due to the fact that he was well known in New Hampshire since, as governor of Massachusetts, he was on the news a lot. The TV stations in the Boston area are seen in the populous area of southern New Hampshire.

Many felt that Dukakis, as a governor, had too little foreign policy and military experience. He tried to overcome that deficiency by putting on an Army tank driver's helmet and having photos taken as he drove around in a tank while standing in the turret with the hatch open. This laughable stunt, of course, did nothing to dispel concern about his lack of military and foreign experience.

Massachusetts, like many states, had a prison furlough program that allowed prisoners to take short leaves. In 1976, the Massachusetts legislature was concerned that prisoners with first-degree murder convictions were allowed to participate in this program, so they passed a law to prevent such prisoners from taking part. Governor Dukakis vetoed it during his first term as governor. During his second term as governor, a prisoner with a life sentence for murder was allowed a furlough. While on this furlough, the prisoner committed armed robbery and rape. Atwater insured that voters were constantly made aware of this by showing an ad with dangerous looking men going around and around in a revolving door (which symbolized the furlough program).

Dukakis was also hurt by the moderator of the second debate, CNN's Bernard Shaw, who began by asking a "gotcha" question. He asked "If your wife, Kitty Dukakis, was raped and murdered, would you favor the death penalty for the killer?" Dukakis was trapped; he could either seem callous toward his wife by not wanting to kill the killer, or reverse his position on the death penalty. Dukakis chose not to rise to the bait and gave a calm, reasoned answer explaining why he did not favor the death penalty. People expected him to react with emotion, so this hurt him.

(This is an example of why media people should not moderate and be the questioners in debates. They are too interested in tripping up the candidates and improving their ratings.)

What Was on Voters' Minds—the Profiles

1988 H.W. Bush Profile

◄──── Unfavorable   Favorable ────►

Government Experience; Record
Poor performance | Experienced, good administrator

Experience in Foreign Affairs

Defense Policy
Too much spending on weapons | Favors strong military

Abortion issue

"He's a Republican"

Association with Reagan ("Gipper" factor)
Too close to Reagan and his policies | Would continue Reagan policies

Strength of Leadership
Weak, uninspiring; a wimp |

Choice of VP running mate

The Campaign
Dirty, negative campaign |
Not addressing the real issues

Group references
He's against working people, the poor |
For big business, the rich |

Involved in Iran-Contra

-10%   0   10%   20%   30%

Percent of Voters who mentioned item

The budget deficit, which had been greatly increased under Reagan, was of great concern to nearly half of the voters in 1988. (See Tables on Issue Publics in Chapter 3.) Yet neither candidate paid much attention to it.

Bush's experience was a major plus for him—he was seen as a good administrator, experienced in foreign affairs, and as favoring a strong military. However, he had almost as many negatives. He was seen as a weak, uninspiring leader; as running a dirty campaign (thanks to Atwater); and as being

1988 Dukakis Profile

Unfavorable ←   Favorable →

Group references

He is for working people; the poor

Social issues

Disapprove of his social welfare,   Approve of his social welfare,
health insurance policies   health insurance, education, day care policies

"He's a Democrat"

The Campaign

Negative, attack campaign
hasn't said anything   Good speaker; good campaign

Tax policy

His position on the Death Penalty

Defense policy

Not for maintaining miliary strength   Agree with his military spending position

Lack of experience in Foreign Affairs

"He's a liberal"

Abortion issue

Government Experience; Record

Lacks experience at notional level
Poor performance as Governor of Mass.   Experienced; good record

Furlough issue

20%   10%   0   10%   20%

Percent of Voters who mentioned item

against working people and the poor and for business and the rich. His choice of running mate (Quayle) also hurt him. But it was his association with Reagan ("The Gipper") and, explicitly, his perceived involvement in the Iran–Contra scandal that hurt him the most.

Dukakis had even more negatives. His lack of experience in foreign affairs, and his defense policy hurt him. Small clusters of people did not like his positions on the death penalty, on taxes, nor abortion (The Atwater attacks worked). The furlough issue was quite damaging. About 7 percent dislike him because he was a liberal, but many more liked his social welfare, health insurance, and day care policies along with his favoring of working people and the poor. The negative views of Dukakis outweighed the positives and that helped Bush get elected, as we will see in Chapter 5.

1996: Clinton vs. Dole

Robert Dole was 73 years old when the 1996 campaign began. He was a World War II veteran who had been wounded and had a lame arm as a result. He had served in Congress for 35 years and had been Senate Majority Leader since 1985. He was one of the last moderate Republicans in congressional leadership positions. In his acceptance speech at the Republican nominating convention, he said, "In politics honorable compromise is no sin. It is what protects us from absolutism and intolerance." Dole's campaign themes were honor, decency, and straight talk. His main policy proposal was to lower income tax rates by 15 percent across the board.

Clinton

Conditions in 1996 were very favorable for an incumbent president seeking re-election. The economy was booming with high employment and low inflation. And we were at peace.

Furthermore, Clinton had accomplished a great deal in this first four years:

Domestic Policies
- Family Medical Leave Act—required companies to provide workers with up to three months of unpaid leave for family and medical emergencies.
- "Don't ask, don't tell"—Gays could serve in the military as long as they did not make their sexual orientation known.
- Omnibus Budget Reconciliation Bill—laid out a plan to cut the budget deficit by a substantial amount by 1998 by a combination of spending cuts and tax increases. (The plan worked and there was a budget surplus the last two years of Clinton's presidency.)
- Vice President Gore headed a National Performance Review (known as "reinventing government.")—It streamlined government, cutting the number of government employees and reducing spending.
- Brady Act—required gun purchasers to have background checks.

- Violent Crime Control and Law Enforcement Act—provided for 100,000 police and more severe penalties of violent crime, including "three strikes and you're out."
- A subsection of the Violent Crime Act prohibited the manufacture of assault weapons for civilian use as well as large capacity magazines. (This section contained a sunset provision and the law expired in September 2004. It was not renewed.)
- Welfare (Aid to Dependent Children) was restructured. It required mothers to work in order to receive aid and made it more difficult to stay on welfare. It was called "Welfare to Work."
- Direct student loans—students could get loans from the government rather than private banks.
- Americare—a corps of volunteers who would perform good works, similar to the Peace Corp but domestic.

Trade
- General Agreement on Tariffs and Trade (GATT) —an agreement among 117 nations to lower tariffs by a third on a wide range of products thus creating freer international markets for goods.
- North American Free Trade Agreement (NAFTA)—an agreement among the United States, Canada, and Mexico to lower barriers to trade.

International
- Mogadishu, Somalia. President G. W. Bush had sent troops to Mogadishu as part of a UN force to bring aid to war-torn and famine ridden Somalia. They were still there when Clinton became president. Two American helicopters were shot down, eighteen American troops were killed and eighty-four wounded trying to rescue the crews. Clinton immediately withdrew our troops from Mogadishu.
- SALT 1. A treaty with Russia that greatly reduced the nuclear warheads of both countries.
- Bringing peace to Bosnia. For years, Clinton did not get U.S troops involved in the ethnic war in Bosnia. He did finally have U.S. bombers bomb Serbia. That was enough to get the Serbs to the bargaining table and our Ambassador, Holbrooke, brokered a peace agreement among the warring parties.

But one thing that Clinton had promised to do in the 1992 campaign—provide health care insurance—had not been accomplished. Early in his presidency, Hillary Clinton had been assigned to come up with a health plan. She and various experts met behind closed doors and finally came up with a plan. It was a complex plan, difficult to explain in a few words. The health insurance industry mounted a major public relations campaign to discredit it. There were the famous Harry and Louise ads, which showed a couple sitting at their kitchen table discussing the proposed plan. They appeared to be reading the plan and remarked, for example, that there would be less coverage and no choice. But the major obstacle was Congress. They did not appreciate being left out of the planning discussions and then handed a package to vote on. Health care died in Congress.

In the 1994 off-year congressional election, the Republicans won a massive victory, gaining control of the House for the first time in forty years. Health care was the main issue cited in the ANES surveys; voters were very disappointed that Clinton had not been able to follow through on his promise. Another factor in the Republican victory was Newt Gingrich, a skilled strategist. He became the Speaker of the House.

Gingrich and Clinton did not get along, and this became a very serious problem especially when it came time to pass budgets. Gingrich threatened to close down the government if he did not get his way. Clinton stood his ground and did not agree to include Gingrich's budget proposals. There was a brief, five-day, shutdown in 1995, but a major one, of twenty-one days, in 1996. Polls showed that most people blamed the Republicans and anger mounted as the twenty-one-day shutdown dragged on. Finally, Gingrich capitulated.

The Accusations

Throughout his first term in office, President Clinton was hounded by the effort on the part of some Republicans to defame him. His problems stemmed from a land purchase he and Hillary made back in 1978. A distant friend, James McDougal, wanted to develop some scenic land next to the White Water river in the Ozarks—an ideal vacation spot for northerners and for retirement homes. McDougal persuaded the Clintons to invest in it. In ensuing years, McDougal bought a small savings and loan bank and used money from it to make fraudulent investments. McDougal was indicted in 1989 for these frauds, but not convicted. These investments had nothing to do with the Whitewater project, which had failed.

Suddenly, in September 1992, the U.S. attorney in Arkansas, received a totally unexpected "referral" from a federal government investigator who insisted that it be acted on "urgently." The referral, inexplicably, listed Bill and Hillary Clinton as "potential witnesses" even though they had no knowledge of McDougal's activities since the Whitewater project years ago, and they had severed all ties to him in 1986. This referral came just before the 1992 election in which the incumbent president, George W. Bush, was Clinton's opponent. The investigator who had sent the urgent referral had been appointed by Bush. Now the Clintons were linked with McDougal because they had been named in the referral. Bill Clinton was elected anyway, but this bogus scandal followed him and Hillary into the White House.

Several of Hillary Clinton's colleagues at the Rose Law Firm, where she had worked, were asked to come to the White House to assist the President on legal matters. One of them was Vince Foster who was given the position of deputy counsel. For some reason, he was immediately the subject of criticism from the media, especially the newly created all-news TV channels. He was bombarded with absurd questions like "was Hillary throwing lamps at the Secret Service" and were he and Hillary having an affair? Even the venerable *Wall Street Journal* joined the attack with an editorial that implied that Foster was an unscrupulous shyster. An experienced Washington hand said, "even Washington pros were surprised at the level of attack. It started from day one."[3]

Vince Foster became very despondent and felt he was a failure. Friends and acquaintances saw a broken man. He committed suicide. Rather than feeling remorse for their bullying, the media questioned whether it was really a suicide. At one point, Hillary Clinton was accused of murdering him. There was a search of his office for a suicide note and, while searching, a box was discovered with some Whitewater papers in it. This should not have been surprise since Forster used to be a member of the Rose Law Firm that years before had given legal representation to McDougal. But the discovery once again put questions about the Whitewater deal on the front burner.

Bill Clinton thought that the only way to put these matters to rest and stop the constant harassment was to appoint an independent council to look into the facts and present evidence. He asked his Attorney General, Janet Reno, to make the appointment. She found a highly qualified and judicious man, Robert Fiske. His charge was to look into Whitewater, the Foster death, and a number of McDougal's frauds. After a few months, Fiske had wrapped up some of his work and filed a report that found strong evidence that Vince Forster had, indeed, committed suicide and no evidence that "issues involving Whitewater or other personal legal matters of president Clinton or Mrs. Clinton were a factor in Foster's suicide."

This conclusion was not well received by those Republicans who were counting on the Clintons being charged with some kind of wrongdoing. About this time, a new independent council authorization bill had been passed and Fiske's appointment had to be renewed under it. Ordinarily, this would have been routine. Technically, the independent counsel is appointed by a special three-judge court after being given suggestions from the Attorney General. Everyone in the Justice Department thought Fiske was doing a fine job and Janet Reno just assumed he would be reappointed. This did not happen. The special three-judge court is appointed by the Chief Justice of the Supreme Court who, at that time, was the very conservative William Rehnquist. He removed the current presiding judge of the special court, George MacKinnon. McKinnon believed that anyone they appointed as an independent counsel should have no connection with either political party. Rehnquist chose someone known to be a partisan Republican to replace MacKinnon. There already was another strongly partisan Republican on the special three-judge court. They chose Ken Starr to replace Fiske.

(When he became independent counsel, Starr continued the ongoing investigation of McDougal. Finally, in 1997, McDougal was indicted and convicted of eighteen felonies. These had to do with financial fraud committed by McDougal. The Clintons were found to be totally innocent of any wrongdoing.)

Starr had already made up his mind about a constitutional issue that would be central to an upcoming investigation—the Paula Jones case. Before being appointed, he had been in consultation with Jones' lawyers and had stated on the MacNeil/Lehrer NewsHour that the president could be sued in a civil case. Democratic Senator Levin, who headed the subcommittee overseeing independent counsel matters, strongly objected to the Starr appointment.

In early January 1994, the far-right tabloid, *The Spectator,* published an unverified exposé about President Clinton's sexual exploits when he was governor of Arkansas. The women mentioned in the article remained anonymous except for one named Paula. A friend of Paula's saw the story and told Paula about it. Paula was highly embarrassed and began to search for ways to clear her name. The incident happened when she was a state employee who was manning a booth at a conference. She was told that the Governor (Clinton) wanted to meet with her in his hotel room. She went up to the room and the rest is "he said, she said." She claimed that Clinton made several sexual advances toward her and asked for a sexual favor. She said she had rejected all of them.

Paula was invited to the annual meeting of the Conservative Political Action Conference (CPAC) where she told her story. Two experienced lawyers—one was an "unabashed Republican" and the other had worked in the Reagan administration—volunteered to help Paula pro bono. Clinton continued to refuse to apologize and to admit he had made unwanted sexual advances.

Jones' lawyers filed a civil law suit against Clinton in the U.S. District Court in Little Rock seeking $700,000 in damages for "willful, outrageous, and malicious conduct at the Excelsior Hotel in Little Rock on May 8, 1991." The District judge, Susan Webber Wright, ruled that any trial should be stayed to the end of Clinton's presidency, but that discovery (finding witnesses and evidence) could go forward.[4] This was in line with a constitutional principle best stated by Judge Joseph Story in 1833:

> There are...incidental powers, belonging to the executive department, which are necessarily implied from the nature of the functions, which are confided to it. Among these, must necessarily be included

the power to perform them, without any obstruction or impediment whatsoever. The President cannot, therefore, be liable to arrest, imprisonment, or detention, while he is in the discharge of the duties of his office...

(One might add another impediment: that is being required to pay damages as result of a civil suit. How is a president going to raise that money without obligating oneself to donors?)

Jones appealed the Wright ruling, but no decision was reached on the appeal until after the 1996 election.

I have taken the time to give a detailed account of the accusations against Clinton since they were highly publicized in the media and made Clinton look bad. These accusations were clearly orchestrated by some Republicans seeking to do harm to the president (Jones made the incident public at an CPAC meeting and her lawyers were Republicans willing to contribute their time for free). We will see in Clinton's profile a large number of negative comments about Clinton that were based on Whitewater and Paula Jones.

What Was on Voters' Minds—the Profiles

1996 Bob Dole Profile

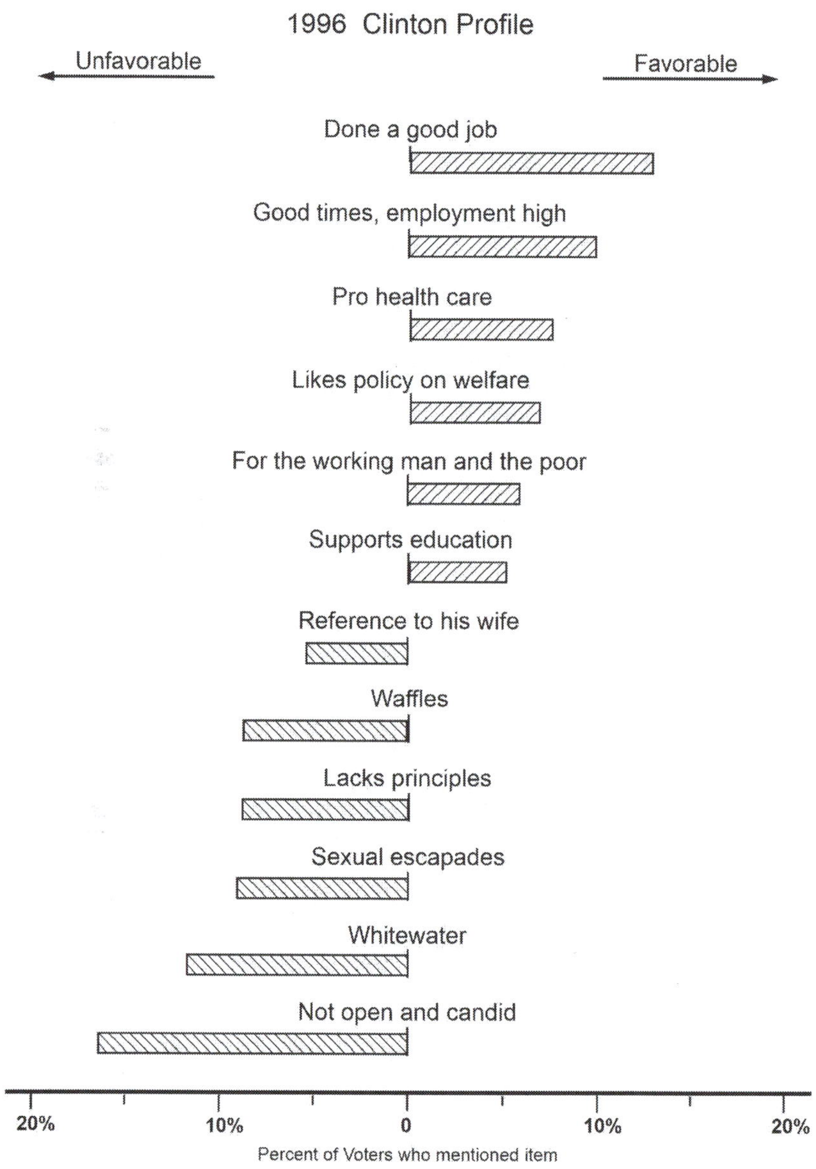

1996 Clinton Profile

Unfavorable ← → Favorable

Done a good job

Good times, employment high

Pro health care

Likes policy on welfare

For the working man and the poor

Supports education

Reference to his wife

Waffles

Lacks principles

Sexual escapades

Whitewater

Not open and candid

20% 10% 0 10% 20%

Percent of Voters who mentioned item

As expected, Dole's age was a major negative. This was balanced by a consideration of Dole's government experience, his honesty and sincerity, and the fact he was a veteran. His promise to lower taxes also appealed to 6 percent of the respondents.

Clinton was thought by many to have done a good job and had brought good times—peace and prosperity. They also liked his "welfare to work" policy and the fact he was in favor of providing health insurance. Many of his policy achievements, such as Family Medical Leave, streamlining government, direct student loans, free trade (NAFTA), and bringing peace to Bosnia, received almost no attention. Most notable was the fact that gun control—the Brady Bill and the ban on assault rifles—aroused little concern. They were mentioned by only a handful.

The effect of the attacks engineered by some Republicans to discredit Bill and Hillary Clinton—the accusations about Whitewater and the death of Vincent Foster—did a lot of damage to both of the Clintons (see negative references to "Whitewater" and negative "references to his wife" in the profiles). The Paula Jones saga is reflected in the comments about Bill Clinton's "sexual escapades." And Clinton's attempts to deny or deflect these charges are reflected in the comments like: "Not open and candid" and "lacks principles."

Clinton barely emerged with a few more positive comments than negative. Had he been opposed by a stronger candidate; the Republican attacks would have resulted in getting rid of him in 1996.

Postscript: The attacks on President Clinton continued into his second term with the advent of the Monica Lewinsky scandal. It led to impeachment by the House of Representatives on December 19, 1998. This was just *after* the 1998 election in which the Democrats picked up many seats in the House, but not enough to constitute a majority. This impeachment had a major effect on the 2000 election, as we will see.

2000: Gore vs. George W. Bush

The 2000 election pitted two mild-mannered men against each other. Al Gore had been Bill Clinton's vice president and George W. Bush was the son of a former president (George H. W. Bush) and was currently governor of Texas. They were not far apart on the issues and Bush advertised himself as a "compassionate conservative." In the debates, Gore seemed ill-at-ease and was reticent, and Bush was more relaxed and natural.

Bush was known to have been a heavy drinker up to the age of forty when he quit for good. A few days before the election, it was discovered that years earlier, in 1976, Bush had been charged with DUI. There is no way to directly see the impact of this news on voters' attitudes since very few interviews were conducted by ANES that close to the election. But it is very interesting to note that those voters who decided late in 2000 contributed 3.5 percent to Gore's total vote. This is why Gore came so close to winning. (See components data in the Chapter 5.) Some criticized Bush for evading going to Vietnam by joining the Texas Air National Guard and serving only locally. He also was known for his malapropisms, mangling word such as saying "strategery" when he meant "strategy."

Gore was known for several things (other than being Clinton's vice president). He advocated a "lock box" for Social Security trust funds. For years, the fund was borrowed from to help fund the regular budget; it ended up being a pile of IOUs, which would be paid back when they came due with more borrowing. There was no cash on hand to invested and help the fund grow. Gore was concerned about this problem and urged that we "lock" the fund away in a hypothetical "box" so Congress could not get its hands on it. (Nothing ever came of this proposal.)

Gore was criticized for sometimes using his office in the White House to raise money, and he was also accused of visiting a Buddhist temple to raise money. One of the biggest problems was that he was accused of saying the he had invented the Internet. This was a result of a pre-interview comment made to CNN's Wolf Blitzer when Gore was talking about his many accomplishments when he was in Congress. One accomplishment, said Gore, was that he helped *create* (not "invent") the Internet. Gore was referring to a bill he got passed in 1991—a bill with his name on it—that funded high-performance computing and technological innovations in communication. That funding helped develop (create) the Internet.

The biggest problem for Gore in 2000 was that he had been Clinton's vice president. The last two years of Clinton presidency were mired in scandal and impeachment. A Special Counsel, Kenneth Starr, had been appointed to investigate allegation of sexual harassment by Clinton when he was governor of Arkansas. During this investigation, Starr learned of inappropriate sexual activity in the Oval Office involving Clinton and a young intern, Monica Lewinsky. Starr asked her to appear before a grand jury. When Clinton heard of this, he is alleged to have called Lewinsky and asked her, when she testified, to deny anything happened. Later, in interviews with the FBI, she was persuaded to tell the truth. When Clinton went before the grand jury, he claimed that "he had never had sexual relations" with Lewinsky.

On December 19, 1998, just *after* the off-year congressional election, the House of Representatives impeached Clinton for obstruction of justice (telling Lewinsky to lie) and perjury (lying about "sexual relations"). However, the Senate acquitted him. Nonetheless, Clinton had been impeached, which told the American public that he was guilty of serious wrongdoing and anyone associated with him was also tainted.

This scandal hung over the White House as the 2000 election approached. Gore decided to distance himself from Clinton as much as possible, even moving his campaign headquarters to Tennessee, and never mentioning anything that he had done while vice president.

What Was on Voters' Minds—the Profiles

Voters had little to say about either candidate in 2000. Many comments were made by just 2 or 3 percent of respondents, not enough to record in the profiles. The major thing said about Bush was that he was honest and sincere—8 percent mentioned this as a favorable trait, but 5 percent thought he did not possess these qualities.

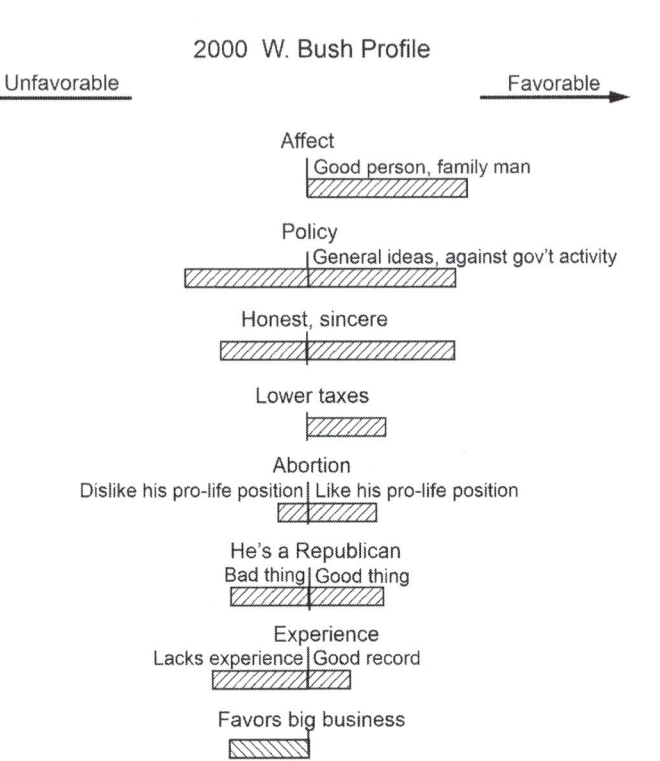

2000 W. Bush Profile

Unfavorable ← → Favorable

Affect
Good person, family man

Policy
General ideas, against gov't activity

Honest, sincere

Lower taxes

Abortion
Dislike his pro-life position | Like his pro-life position

He's a Republican
Bad thing | Good thing

Experience
Lacks experience | Good record

Favors big business

Intelligence
Unintelligent, poor at explaining

20%   10%   0   10%   20%
Percent of Voters who mentioned item

Seven percent liked Gore because of his government experience, but 4 percent criticized him for being part of the Washington crowd. A considerable number, 10 percent, did not like the fact that he was close to Clinton, the impeached president. The largest set of negative comments (13 percent) appeared under the code category "dishonest and insincere, not straightforward." It is hard to know what that was referring to. Only 3 percent specifically mentioned the claim that he had "invented" the Internet. The way he raised campaign funds was only mentioned by 3 percent as well.

The contest between Gore and Bush ended in a virtual tie, which was decided by a month-long recount of the Florida vote. It ended with Bush having a few hundred more votes than Gore in Florida. The Electoral Votes of Florida gave Bush enough to win. The results would have been different if Gore had not had ten percent of the voters against him because of his association with the impeached president.

2000 Gore Profile

← Unfavorable   Favorable →

Past experience
Professional politician | Was Senator, Vice President

Aid to aged, Increase Social Security

Affect
| Good man, family man

Aid to Education

Environment

He's a Democrat

Character
Weak, indecisive, uninspiring |

Abortion
He is pro-choice |

Being Close to Clinton
Negative | Positive

Charges against him
Soliciting at Buddhist Temple |
Claim to have invented Internet |

Sincerity
Not straight forward, evasive | Honest, sincere

20%   10%   0   10%   20%

Percent of Voters who mentioned item

2004: George W. Bush vs. John Kerry

The 2004 election was the first presidential election after the terrorist attack of 9/11. President Bush had been a strong and expressive leader in the days after the attack. He had also had two major legislative achievements: No Child Left Behind (2001) and Medicare prescription drug coverage (2003). He also cut taxes.

But then he invaded Iraq to bring down Saddam Hussein who was thought to be building nuclear weapons. (It was found out after we invaded that there was no nuclear program.) Iraq was totally destabilized without a strong leader and our troops were caught in the middle of a fight between the two major religious sects, the Shia and the Sunni. The fighting was raging as the 2004 election approached and there was no end in sight. However, the largest problem in the public's mind in 2004 was terrorism—42 percent cited it as the Most Important Problem.

Kerry

John Kerry was a Vietnam War veteran who had commanded a swift boat, a small boat used to patrol inland waters. His bravery and quick thinking got his men through some very harrowing situations and he was awarded a Silver Star and a Bronze Star. He was also wounded and twice received a Purple Heart. He was very troubled by atrocities committed by some of our troops, and when he returned home he joined the Vietnam Veterans Against the War and appeared before the Senate Foreign Relations Committee in 1971 and apprised the committee of the atrocities.

In 1973, Kerry got a law degree and went on to earn a J.D. in 1976. For several years thereafter, he worked as a prosecuting attorney for the State of Massachusetts. In 1982 he was elected Lt. Governor and then went on the U.S. Senate in 1985. He initiated no major legislation.

In 2003, Kerry began his quest for the presidency.[5] He was fuzzy on the issues, seeing the complexity and nuance of each issue and unable to state a clear position. He had no core set of issues that concerned him, no convictions, and his style was stilted and aloof. Thus, he was particularly reliant on advisors to help formulate positions and improve his speaking ability.

From the outset, he had staffing problems. He was not doing well in the early primaries and blamed his campaign manager, whom he fired. He then took on a group of advisors who had worked for Ted Kennedy—Mary Beth Cahill as campaign manager and Stephanie Cutter as communications director. A longtime Democratic strategist, Bob Shrum, was also a major overall influence on campaign strategy. All of this staff had strong personalities and vied to be the one who determined the style of Kerry's campaign and the issues he would address. The situation was described as a "chaotic battlefield of multiple feuding tribes."[6]

As the campaign progressed, Kerry became worn-down by his squabbling staff. He was also getting very bad advice (some of which will be described shortly). The crew of advisors, especially James Carville, who had help Clinton win the presidency in 1992, became alarmed with Kerry's floundering campaign. They simply stepped in and filled key positions on

Kerry's staff including a prominent role for Joe Lockhart who had been Clinton's Press Secretary.

Even though the Iraq War was of major concern to over half of the voters, Kerry took no position on it. This ambivalence on the Iraq War created a monumental problem for him. In 2002, Kerry (then a senator) had voted to authorize the ""use of force, if necessary, to disarm Saddam Hussein." In 2003, the President asked Congress for a supplemental authorization of $87 billion to fund the troops in Iraq. There was an alternative bill under consideration which would allow for the authorization if President Bush would rescind some of this tax cuts in order to pay for it. Kerry voted for this alternative. When that failed, he decided to vote against the spending of $87 billion. At a campaign rally, when asked why he had voted against supporting our troops, he replied "I actually did vote for the $87 billion before I voted against it." This awkward wording was reported as "First I voted for it, then I voted against it." This made him look like a flip-flopper on the overall question of invading Iraq, not just whether to approve the supplemental appropriation. (The Bush campaign kept reminding voters of it by showing an ad of Kerry on a windsurfer tacking to-and-fro.) Then, at another rally, when he was asked if he would have voted to invade Iraq whether it had Weapons of Mass Destruction (WMDs) or not. His campaign manager, Cahill, advised him to say "yes". Now he was saying he supported invasion for the sake of invasion. Voters saw a candidate who did not know where he stood on Iraq.

At the beginning of August, a campaign ad sponsored by the Swift Boat Veterans for Truth began to appear, which attacked Kerry for his "betrayal" of our troops in Vietnam when he testified before the Senate Foreign Relations Committee back in 1971. They also said he had not been wounded, had not earned his medals, and was not respected by his crew. The ads were well produced and included many pictures of men who claimed to be veterans. Kerry's advisor, Shrum, recommended that Kerry should not "dignify" the ads by responding to them. Other advisors said it would be a mistake for him to hit back because voters do not like negative campaigning and mudslinging.[7] "Better to float above it all," they said. The ads were shown again and again, rebroadcast for free by cable news channels. With no reply from Kerry, many in the public believed they must be true. At one point, someone in the Kerry entourage suggested he get his boat crew together and show their support for him publicly, but the idea was rejected. Their support might have meant the difference between Kerry winning or losing.

What Was on Voters' Minds—the Profiles

After the 9/11 terrorist attack on the World Trade Center and the Pentagon, the overwhelming concern of the public in 2004 was terrorism (with 42 percent citing it as an issue). The two major positive views of Bush were that he was

2004 Kerry Profile

◄——— Unfavorable   Favorable ———►

His opponent
Ran against someone I really disliked

He's a Democrat

Intelligent, will do a good job

The Economy
Economy better with Kerry

Government Health Program

Handle Iraq situation

Service in Viet Nam
Questions service in Viet Nam | War record, served in Viet Nam

Statements about Vietnam Vets

Too liberal

Sincerity
Breaks promises, not straightforward | Honest, sincere

Record
Poor record in Senate
Part of Washington crowd

Campaign
Poor campaign, too negative

Strength of Leadership
Weak, indecisive, vacillating, uninspiring | Strong leader

30%   20%   10%   0   10%

Percent of Voters who mentioned item; Last-minute Deciders not included

handling the problem of terrorism well and that he showed strong leadership by being decisive. They saw Bush as a president who would prevent any further attacks. However, a great many, 46 percent, were critical of his invasion of Iraq.

A secondary issue was the economy. Fourteen percent criticized Bush for not dealing with it while about an equal number thought Kerry would do a better job.

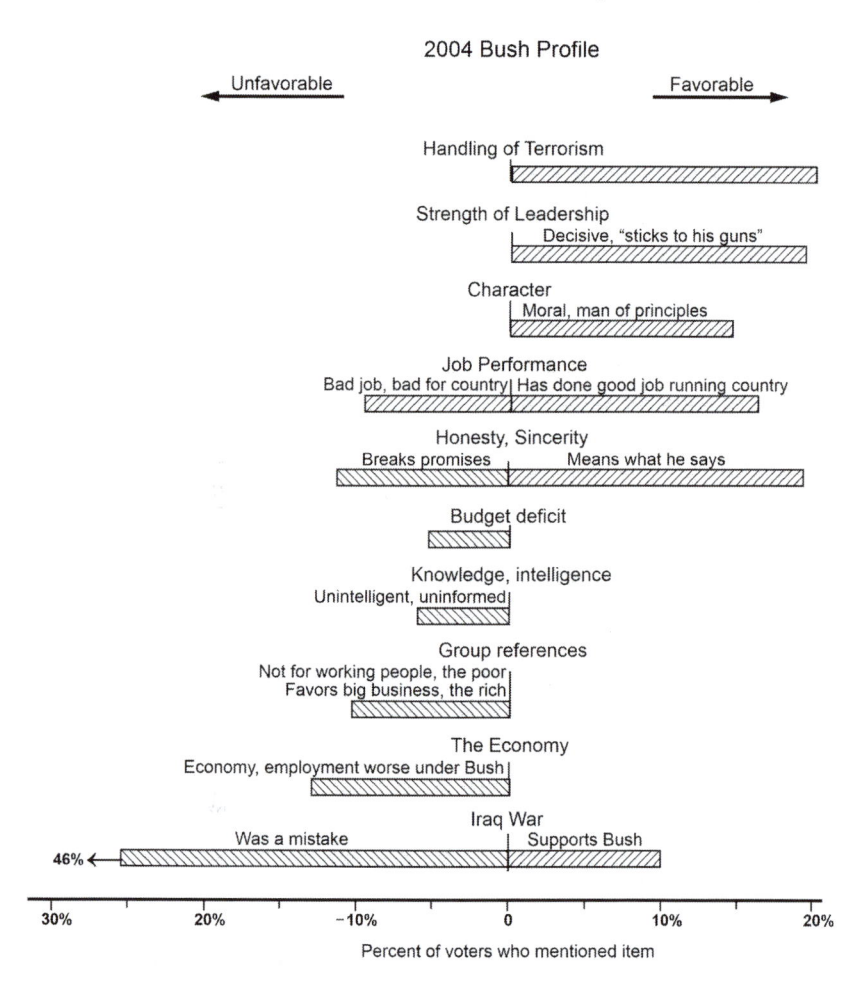

2004 Bush Profile

Percent of voters who mentioned item

Kerry

There were two major factors in Kerry's favor: (1) many disliked Bush more than Kerry and (2) he was a Democrat—two things that any Democratic candidate would have benefited from. The only substantive issues Kerry was credited for was favoring government health insurance.

Being a veteran is usually a plus for a candidate, but in Kerry's case just as many questioned Kerry's service in Vietnam as praised him for it. His 1971 appearance before a Congressional committee criticizing some of the actions of our troops in Vietnam was specifically mentioned by 6 percent. The Swift boat ads also had hurt him badly.

Kerry's flip-flopping and uncertainty on the Iraq War drew an unusually large number of negative comments. Many saw him as someone who breaks promises and is not straightforward. Over 30 percent thought Kerry was weak, indecisive, or vacillating. His ever-changing staff was never able to give him consistency and direction and the public had a very negative impression of his campaign.

2016: Hillary Clinton vs. Donald Trump

As the 2016 election approached, the economy was quite good—the unemployment rate was 5 percent, the stock market had doubled since the Great Recession of 2008, and consumer confidence was high. However, the GDP was increasing by only 1.9 percent a year and wages were stagnant. Also, many good factory jobs, especially in the Mid-West (Rust Belt), had been outsourced to foreign countries.

For the first time since 9/11, war was not a major problem. There were very few American troops fighting in the Middle East and ISIS was retreating. There were, however. terrorist attacks on civilians in the United States, but mostly in Europe.

Congress had been deadlocked for almost ten years; many problems, such as infrastructure, immigration and global warming, had not been dealt with.

Hillary Clinton

Hillary Clinton had a wealth of experience in the political world and thus was well qualified to be president. She had been the First Lady when Bill Clinton was president, she was twice elected to the U.S. Senate, and became Secretary of State in the Obama administration. But these experiences were also a liability. When she was First Lady, she was subjected to vicious accusations about Whitewater and the death of Vince Foster. Many criticized her for standing by her husband when he was impeached for lying about sexual activities. When Clinton was Secretary of State, she made two bad decisions—she used a private server to handle her official emails and she failed to send marines to Benghazi, Libya to guard State Department officials. Libya was in chaos following the overthrow of Omar Qadhafi and was being overrun by armed militias and Al-Qaeda affiliates. A senior State Department official was killed in an attack on an unguarded consulate in Benghazi.[8]

Republican Congressional committees held several hearings in which they asked Secretary Clinton to explain the Benghazi decision, thus repeatedly reminding the public of the incident. Regarding the server, many experts said that using a private server for official business was possibly illegal and definitely dangerous for national security—it could be hacked. The explanations Clinton made about both incidents were evasive and unapologetic.[9]

She began the primary campaign with high negatives. Polls in August 2015, for example, showed that large segments of the public thought she was dishonest, a liar, and untrustworthy.[10] The reasons for these attitudes cannot be known. Was it Whitewater and Vince Foster, standing by her husband at impeachment time, or failure to "be straight" with the American people about the emails and Benghazi? We do know that these anti-Clinton attitudes were present long before Trump began to rail against her in the general election campaign. Trump constantly reminded his rallygoers about Clinton by having them shout: "Lock her up" and by constantly referring to her as "Crooked Hillary."

A main feature of Hillary Clinton's campaign was reminding voters that, if elected, she would have broken through the "glass ceiling"—the hypothetical ceiling that kept women from being elected to the highest offices. She was counting on the women's vote.

There were no issues that Clinton was known for. Her approach to issues was incremental and cautious. For example, she was for an increase in the minimum wage but not to for as much as $15 dollars an hour. She was for some help with the cost of higher education, but not totally free tuition.

What Voters Thought about Hillary Clinton—Her Profile

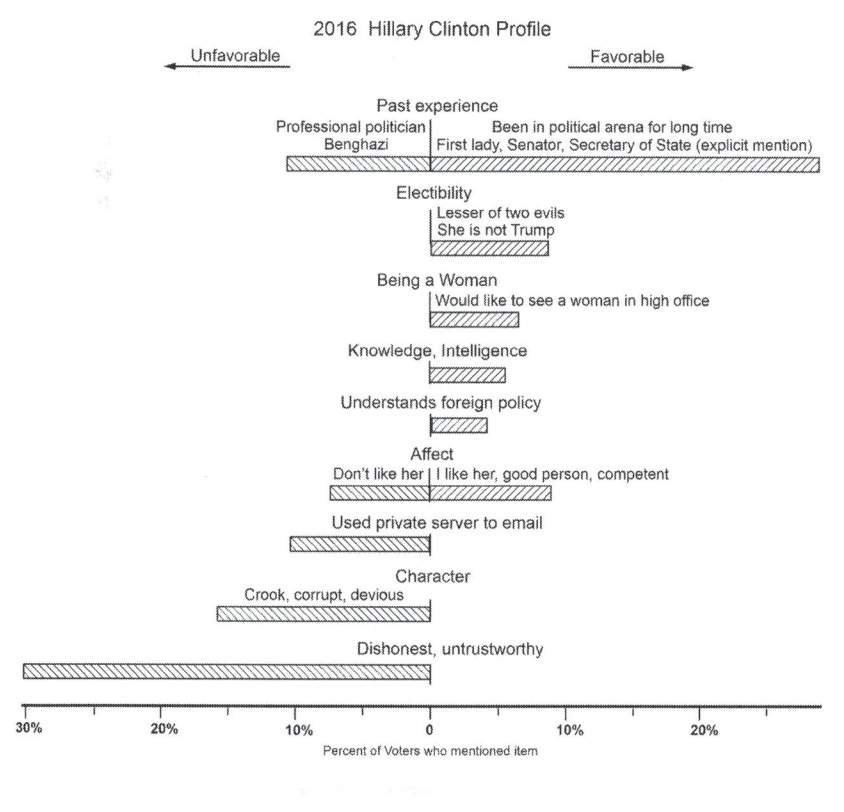

When we look at Clinton's profile, we see one long favorable bar at top and several long unfavorable bars at the bottom. A majority of comments about her were negative. Her experience as First Lady, Senator, and Secretary of State plus her understanding of foreign policy were much in her favor, but her missteps regarding Benghazi and her private email server were also frequently mentioned. A great many saw her as dishonest and untrustworthy. No one commented on her policies; there were none that stood out. Some commented that it would be good to see a woman in high office, but we saw in Chapter 2 that she did not receive an extra boost from women voters overall. There were no negative comments about her being a woman.

Donald Trump

Before the 2016 election campaign, Donald Trump was known for being a very wealthy real estate developer, as the host of a popular TV show called "The Apprentice," and as a leader in the effort to delegitimize President Obama by claiming he was born in Africa. Some people were also aware that he had become bankrupt several times. He had no political experience and most observers, including himself, never thought he could win.

His primary campaign began in the lobby of his New York hotel. Among his first comments was a proposal to build a wall to prevent Mexicans from illegally entering the United States. He said that these immigrants "were bringing drugs and crime, and they are rapists." In this initial speech he announced his major slogan: "Make American Great Again." His bias against Mexicans was made clear throughout his campaign and, at one point, he extended it to a second generation Mexican as well. When a federal judge ruled against him, Trump said the judge was incompetent because his parents came from Mexico.

Trump's attitude toward blacks was made clear by his reaction to black demonstrators at his rallies. At one rally, when a small group of blacks started shouting "Black Lives Matter," Trump shouted back, "Get out" and the crowd cheered. One man said "Niggers go home" and as these blacks were being escorted out, a white man in the audience sucker punched one of them. At another rally, when a Black Lives Matter activist was escorted out peacefully by guards, Trump commented "Maybe he should have been roughed up."

Trump was constantly belligerent toward opponents. He would say things like "knock the crap out of them" or I would "like to punch you in the face." In short, he condoned, even encouraged, violence against minorities and critics.

Trump was a misogynist and he demonstrated it in a number of ways. He insulted women media commentators, including those who were questioning him in the debates. At one point in the campaign, a revealing tape surfaced—Trump was heard having a conversation with a friend in which he bragged about how he gave unwanted kisses to women, and worse, how he had fondled their private parts.

In addition, he tried to intimidate the other candidates in the primaries and invented derogatory names for them. He was ignorant of basic facts and used lies to coverup this deficiency. And he was a prime example of an egotist.

His rallies were well attended, festive events; as much entertainment as they were political—reminiscent of the rallies of southern demagogues of yore such as Huey Long. Trump talked repeatedly about issues neither party was addressing such as illegal immigration, trade agreements (NAFTA), and the outsourcing of jobs. He promised to bring jobs back to America. He railed against power brokers and the political establishment in Washington and promised to "drain the swamp."

What Voters Thought about Trump—His Profile

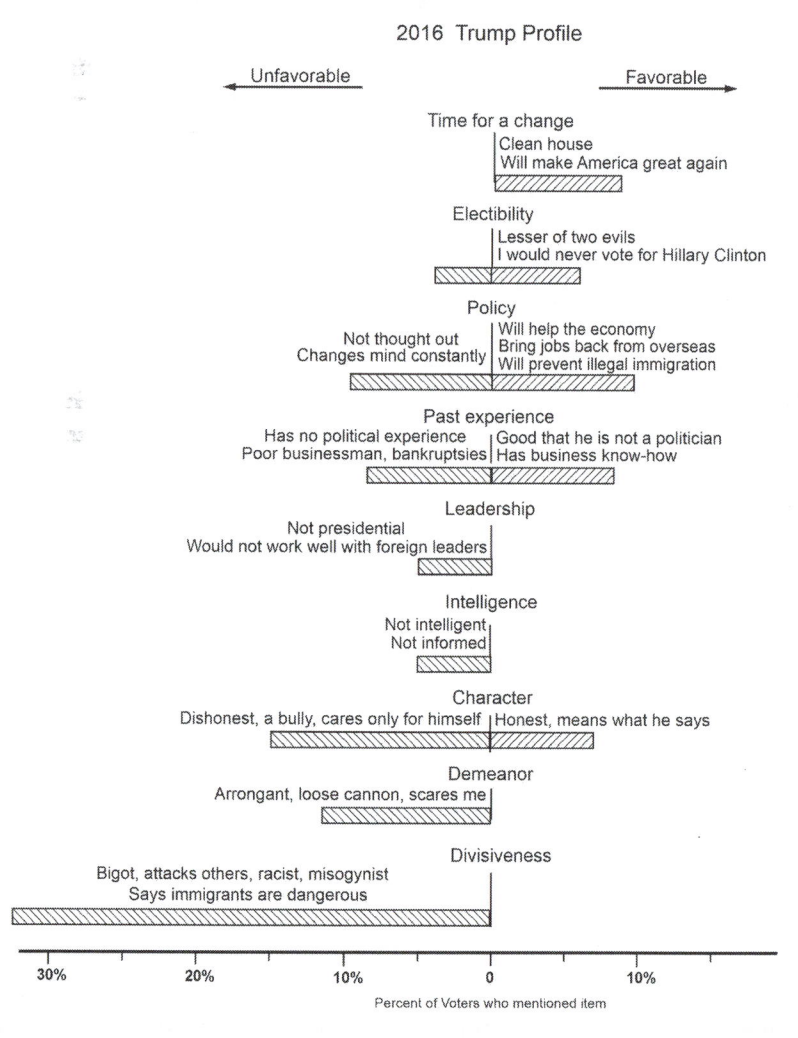

Trump induced an overwhelming number of unfavorable comments; 61 percent of comments about him were negative. Most of this was due to his character (dishonest, a bully, cares only for himself), his demeanor (arrogant, loose cannon, scary), but mostly it was due his divisiveness. He was seen as a racist, a misogynist, and a xenophobe who condoned violence against others. We saw in the issues presented in Chapter 3 that he created national problems—divisiveness and racism were at the top of the list of Issue Publics. Just after his election in November 2016, when asked what the major problems were, quite a few cited Trump himself.

There were a few favorable comments about Trump. His experience as a businessman was seen as a positive—he would bring a businessman's "know how." Some liked the idea that he was not a politician, but an equal number were concerned that he had no political experience. Some were aware that he was not a good businessman because of his bankruptcies. People liked him because he was going to clean house (drain the swamp) in Washington, help the economy, bring back jobs from overseas, and prevent illegal immigration. But despite these clear policies, quite a few saw him as someone who kept changing his mind.

Even the second most positive comment about Trump was not praise for him but rather a dislike of Clinton—comments like "lesser of two evils" or "I would never vote for Hillary Clinton."

And so, in 2016, we had two disliked candidates, with Trump disliked much more than Clinton. To a remarkable extent, even before he became president, a great number of voters "had his number." They saw him as a demagogue, a misogynist, a racist, as divisive, as uninformed, as a liar. The question is: how could a candidate have such exceedingly high unfavorability yet still become president? This question will be answered in Chapter 5.

Summary of Profile Findings

In looking over the profiles, one sees an electorate that does quite a good job evaluating the candidates. Although there are some comments that are non-substantive feelings such as "I like him" and "he is a good person," there are a great many substantive and insightful comments. Voters do not simply look at candidates' personalities and they usually makes judgments based on known qualities. Listed below are the criteria used by most voters to evaluate candidates:

1   The criteria most often used was the policy positions taken by the candidates. There were seventeen specific policies mentioned, seven references to general policy or ideas, four regarding the economy, two with regard to the Vietnam War and two, the Iraq War.

2   An almost universally applied criteria was honesty, sincerity, and "meaning what you say" (authenticity).
3   Record in office and experience was often commented on.
4   Affect—whether the candidate was liked/disliked or thought to be a good/bad person.
5   Evaluation of leadership ability and decisiveness were important criteria.
6   Being a supporter of the common/working man or siding with the rich was often remarked about.
7   And finally, the candidate's character was judged.

Using these criteria, voters make up their own minds about the candidates. There is little evidence that the commentary by media analysts influences their evaluations.

The Missing Mentions: Ideology, Taxes, and Abortion

In any campaign, the ideology of the candidate is thought (by the political elite) to be of major importance in voters' evaluation of the candidates. Also, the issues of taxes and abortion are considered "hot button" issues that candidates must be careful of. But, in fact, voters do not use these items as criteria when judging candidates.

Liberals and Conservatives

Labeling a candidate as a liberal or a conservative is almost always part of the dialog of a campaign, often brought up by a candidate's opponent and the media. Let us look at how many voters mentioned "liberal" or "conservative" when giving their attitudes toward the candidates. "Conservative" was mentioned with regard to Goldwater by 10 percent—4 percent positively and 6 percent negatively. The label "conservative" was not applied to Reagan at all. Only 5 percent disliked McGovern, and 7 percent disliked Dukakis because they were liberal. A net of 6 percent disliked Kerry because he was liberal. Thus, ideology was used to judge candidates in only four of the twenty-two profiles, and when it was mentioned, it was not mentioned by many. Clearly, ideology has little to do *directly* with how voters judge candidates.

Taxes

There were only three elections in which taxes were mentioned in the profiles. Early in his first term, Reagan introduced a massive tax cut. When he ran for re-election in 1984, only 12 percent of voters mentioned it and they were mostly unfavorable, seeing it as benefiting the rich. George W. Bush lowered taxes when he came to office in 2000, but only 4 percent gave him credit for it in the next election (2004).

Thus, we see that lowering taxes has very little pay-off in voter approval. Also, as noted earlier, during the 1988 campaign, H. W. Bush repeatedly said: "read my lips, no new taxes." There was no mention of taxes in Bush's profile.

Mondale was concerned with the large national debt that Reagan had run up, and told the American people that taxes would have to be raised to pay for it. In Mondale's profile we see that 16 percent mentioned taxes: 11 percent negatively and 5 percent positively—a net of 6 percent unfavorable to Mondale. (As noted earlier in viewing Mondale's profile, there were four other criticisms of Mondale that were mentioned far more often.)

In short, taxes are of little interest to most voters. And in Chapter 6 we will see that most voters do not consider taxes to be burdensome. When the ANES asked, "Do you feel you are asked to pay *more* federal tax than you should?" except for the most extreme conservatives, only a third of the electorate felt they were paying more federal tax than they should. And as for the extreme conservatives, only half thought they were taxed more than they should.

Abortion

Abortion has been a perennial issue in campaigns and is thought to be a "third rail" issue that candidates do not dare touch unless they are pro-life. Over all the years of this study, a candidate's position on abortion has almost never been noted by voters. Only in 1988 was it mentioned and then by only 5 percent. Eight percent disliked Dukakis for being pro-choice but 2 percent liked him for it—a net negative of 6 percent. Eight percent liked Bush for his pro-life position but 3 percent dislike him for it—a net of 5 percent approval of Bush on the issue. This is not an impressive impact for an issue that receives so much attention.

Furthermore, in Chapter 3 we saw that abortion was never an issue mentioned as a most important problem and, in Chapter 6, it will be seen that abortion is not part of the belief system of conservatives.

Effect of Topics Frequently Mentioned by the Media

The 3 A's in 1972

McGovern was for <u>a</u>mnesty for those who went to Canada to escape the draft during the Vietnam war, was pro-choice on the <u>a</u>bortion issue, and was for legalizing certain drugs (one of which at the time was called "<u>a</u>cid"). The media labeled these the 3A's and repeatedly referred to that group of issues as a negative factor that could seriously hurt McGovern. Looking over McGovern's profile, you will see none of these issues mentioned.

Ford's Debate Gaffe re: Eastern Europe

In one of the debates in the 1976 campaign, Gerald Ford made the following comment when asked a question about Eastern Europe: "There is no Soviet domination of Eastern Europe and there never will be under a Ford administration." The media immediately jumped on this gaffe and often reminded listeners about it. No respondent in the 1976 ANES survey mentioned it.

Conclusion

Analysts cannot assume that the prominence of an issue in the political elite's dialog will have an impact of voters' decisions.

Age

Ronald Reagan was sixty-nine when he first ran for president. A substantial number of voters (12 percent) were concerned that he was too old. An equal number remained concerned about his age in 1984. A major factor in Bob Dole's defeat in 1996 was his age; he was seventy-three. Seventeen percent mentioned it. Being young (forty-three) was a net asset for Kennedy—10 percent liked the idea of a young president although 6 percent did not.

The Legacy of Being a Vice President

When a candidate had been a vice president, the performance of the president he served under "rubs off" onto the candidate. There were four of these situations: JFK→LBJ, LBJ→HHH, Carter→Mondale, and Clinton→Gore. In 1968, LBJ was very unpopular, yet HHH remained loyal to him and lost. Carter had failed miserably and Mondale paid for it four years later in 1984. Clinton had been impeached and Gore wisely kept his distance from him. Yet voters were well aware that Gore had been close to Clinton. Being associated with an impeached president kept Gore from being elected, as we will see in the next chapter.

The Effect of Ads

Of all the ads that were shown in the campaigns studied in this book, only five had measurable effects.

1   The "Daisy Girl" ad in 1964, which shows a young girl in a field of daisies counting petals as she pulls them one-by-one from the flower. "One, two, three ..." she says, and then her voice fades into a male voice counting "eight, nine, ten, launch" and the mushroom shape of an atomic bomb is seen in the background. The purpose of this ad was to draw attention to Goldwater's risky policies regarding atomic weapons such as giving tactical command of them to generals in Europe and using them in Vietnam. It is hard to say whether it was this ad or Goldwater's speeches in which he often talked about using nuclear weapons, that caused many respondents to remark about Goldwater's "warlike" and "fanatic" tendencies.

2   "The Morning in America" ad in 1984. It was narrated by Ronald Reagan as he showed pictures of families that were so much better off than they were when he took office. He showed that more people had jobs, interest rates were much lower which enable many to buy homes, and inflation was no longer skyrocketing.

3   The "Revolving Door" ad in 1988 showed some dangerous looking men going around and around in a revolving door. It was to remind voters of an incident in Massachusetts while Dukakis was the governor. Massachusetts had a furlough program that allowed prisoners to go home for a weekend. A murdered, Willie Horton, was given a furlough. He committed armed robbery and rape while on furlough. Dukakis was severely criticized for letting this happen. The greatest number of negative comments about Dukakis was the "furlough issue."

4   "The Windsurfer" ad in 2004 in which Kerry is on a windsurfer tacking to-and-fro. This was to remind voters of Kerry's remark about his position on the Vietnam War: "first I was for it, then I was against it." In the profiles we see that a very large set of voters thought he was "weak," "indecisive," or "vacillating."

The four ads mention above did not create issues that were not already there. It was Goldwater himself who kept talking about nuclear war; the furlough issue was based on a real event that Dukakis could have prevented had he not vetoed a bill that would have prevented a murderer from being on furlough; and Kerry was always changing positions on the Iraq War. The ads simply repeated and dramatized these issues so voters would not forget them.

Then there were the ""Swift Boat" ads. Kerry was the commander of a swift boat during the Vietnam War. When he came home, he appeared before a congressional committee and spoke of the terrible things that were happening there. A group of Vietnam veterans, offended by what Kerry had said, prepared several ads demeaning Kerry—saying he did not deserve the medals he had received, that he was a poor commander, and his men disliked him. Much of what the ads said was untrue and from then on, if a candidate was a victim of false-negative ads, he or she was thought be "swiftboated." In Kerry's profile we see that 8 percent praised him for his service in Vietnam but that was negated by 8 percent who questioned his service. These false ads did have an effect.

The Media's Role in Showing Ads

One wonders how much impact ads would have if they were only shown when paid for. For example, the well-known "Daisy girl" ad in 1964 was only shown once as a paid ad, but it was shown often on the evening news programs. Would it have been remembered if only shown once? Since then, news programs have often rebroadcast ads for free. This would seem to be a violation of the media's role to report on campaigns, not participate in them. These ads are propaganda and when producers of news program choose which propaganda to put on the air, they are inserting themselves into the campaign by making choices of who to support with favorable ads or who to hurt by showing negative ads.

Notes

1 The EIC (Earned Income tax Credit)—a provision for a tax refund for those with very low incomes—was passed a few years later, in 1975, during the Nixon administration.

2 There was a major influx of women in the workforce, from an average of 38 percent in the ten years before Carter took office to 46 percent by1980.

3 Ken Gormley, *The Death of American Virtue*, p. 70. Much of my information about the Whitewater and Paula Jones saga came from this book.

4 This decision was overturned in a unanimous decision by the Supreme Court in the case of *Clinton v. Jones* in May 1997.

5 A *Newsweek* reporter, Holly Bailey, was allowed to observe the Kerry campaign up-close and personal, taking notes on all conversations as long as she did not publish until after the campaign was over. Much of my information in this section about Kerry came from that reporting. See www.newsweek.com/vets-attack-124775.

6 Quote from Michael Crowley of *Slate*, April 15, 2004.

7 It is difficult to understand how setting the record straight on Kerry's war record could be considered mudslinging.

8 On October 4, 2012, an Accountability Review Board was set up to examine the facts and circumstances of the Benghazi attack. Their report stated that "there were systematic failures and leadership and management deficiencies at senior levels within the State Department that resulted in a special mission security posture that was inadequate for Benghazi."

9 In her autobiography after the 2016 campaign (*What Happened*), Clinton never mentions the server or Benghazi. Apparently, she did not take these criticisms seriously.

10 For example, an August 2015 Quinnipiac poll asked respondents, "What is the first word that comes to mind when you think of Hillary Clinton?" By far, the most mentioned words—45 percent of them—were "liar", "dishonest" and "untrustworthy."

References

Clinton, Hillary Rodham. 2017. *What Happened*. New York: Simon &Schuster.
Gormley, Ken. 2010. *The Death of American Virtue*. New York: Crown Publishers.

5

THE COMPONENTS OF THE VOTE

In the previous chapters we have studied the four components of the electoral decision: attitudes toward the Republican and Democratic candidates, issue concerns, and party identification. In this chapter we will pull together these four components and show the relative importance of each in the overall outcome of elections. We will use the Model Equation, which is a multiple regression equation. Multiple regression equations have two forms—the standardized and the non-standardized. In the standardized version, the original data is converted into values that measure the data in standardized units. Using these units, we can measure the relative importance of each independent variable since the units are comparable. In the Introduction, we wanted to find the *overall weight voters place on each independent variable (component) when making their decision*, so we used the standardized version of the equation.

In this chapter, we will look at the resulting decisions voters made after weighing each component. The bars in Figures 5.1a–5.1d show the net effect of the components in moving the entire electorate in one partisan direction or the other. The effect of each component will be measured separately and then the effect of all components, taken together, will be calculated. The candidate component is based on the result of voters weighing the pros and cons of the candidates. The issue component was based on the partisan valence of the issue cited as the most important. In some elections, party identification influenced the voter's decision, but in others it was less important. The length of the bars in Figure 5.1 show the amount each component benefited or hurt candidates. (A detailed explanation of this can be found in Appendix C.)

To do this, we need to use the original (non-standardize) data and the non-standardized Model Equation. The non-standardized equation looks like this:

$$\text{Vote} = a + b_1\text{DC} - b_2\text{RC} + b_3\text{PID} + b_4\text{MIP}$$

(The non-standardized regression coefficient (weight) is designated by a "b" rather than a "β," which is the symbol of the standardize coefficient or beta weight.)

Note that if a candidate (say, candidate X) has an opponent who is more disliked than liked, that negative attitude toward the opponent benefits candidate X. Therefore, the opponent's component is shown in candidate X's direction. For example, we see in Carter's 1980 profile in Chapter 4 that he had many more negative attitudes than positive. In the 1980 components figure, Carter is shown on the pro-Republican side; indeed he is one of the major reasons Reagan won.

The Non-standardized Multiple Regression Equation

There is a change to all multiple regression equations when we move from the standardized to the non-standardized version. Note the "a" term. This stands for some variable that has not been included in the equation but is necessary if the equation is to accurately predict the dependent variable (the vote). Most researchers pay little attention to this "a" term, but it occurred to me that if we are going to fully explain the results of an election, we must know what the missing variable is. I thought of the equation as a puzzle consisting of five pieces ("a," DC, RC, PID, and MIP). Four of the pieces—DC, RC, PID, and MIP—are found by substituting the original data into the Model Equation and finding the values of b_1, b_2, b_3, and b_4. The fifth (missing) piece is "a" and it would have to be of a certain size and shape to fit into the partially completed puzzle. I searched for a variable of the size and shape that would complete the puzzle. The ANES studies are omnibus and have a great many questions to search among. Using trial and error, I substituted one question at a time into the equation until I found the variable that fit— that is, took the place of the "a" term.[1] (It was not necessary to search for a substitute for the "a" term if the term was insignificant, that is, less than .03.)

I call this "a" term the "adjuvant" factor—something that is added to the equation to replace the "a" term, something to complete the equation. It was something that was at the back of many voters' minds that influenced their vote, perhaps subconsciously.

Another consideration that is necessary to bring accuracy to the Model Equation is the time of decision. The ANES interviews that measure attitudes toward candidates take place during a seven-week period before an election. Those voters who make up their minds a few days before election day may well have

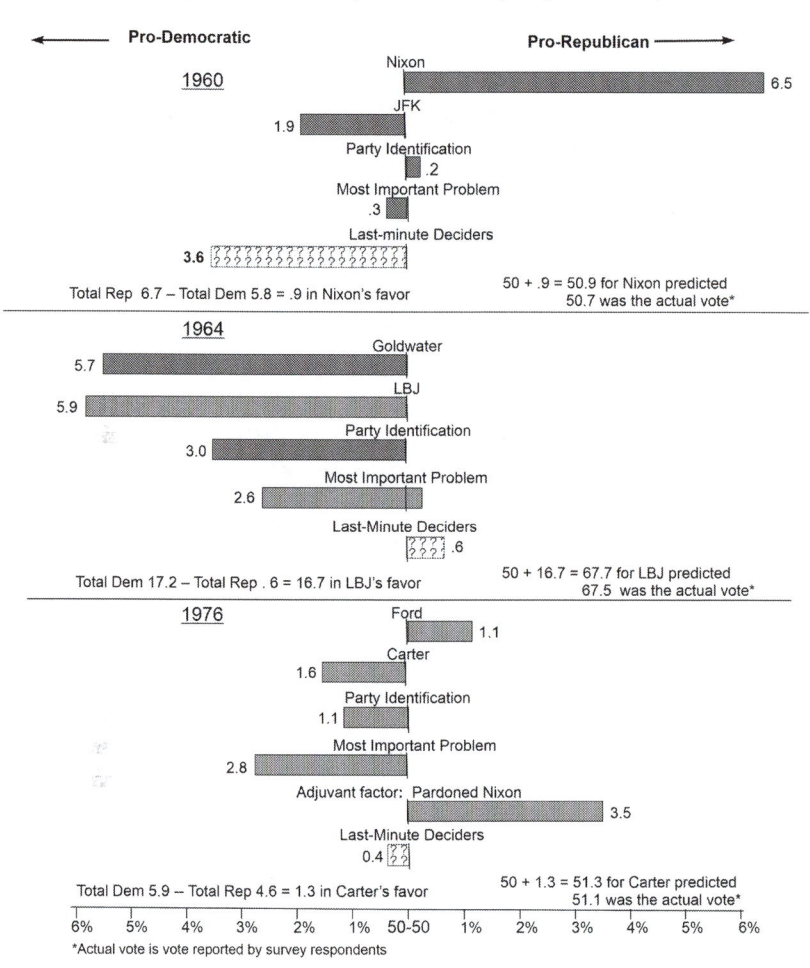

Bar lengths are the mean of component attitudes multiplied by "b" in Model Equation

FIGURE 5.1a Components of Vote, 1960–1976.

changed their attitudes toward the candidates during the campaign, after they had been interviewed. Thus, attitudes measured at an earlier time are not going to be a good predictor of vote for the late-deciders. Therefore, I removed from my regression analyses those respondents who reported making up their minds a few days before the election. Their vote is reported separately (Figures 5.1a–5.1d).

Explanation of Figure 5.1

At the bottom of each year's graphic presentation of bars is shown the calculation of the net effect of all bars taken together. To make this calculation, I looked first for the bars in the favorable direction and totaled them. Then the

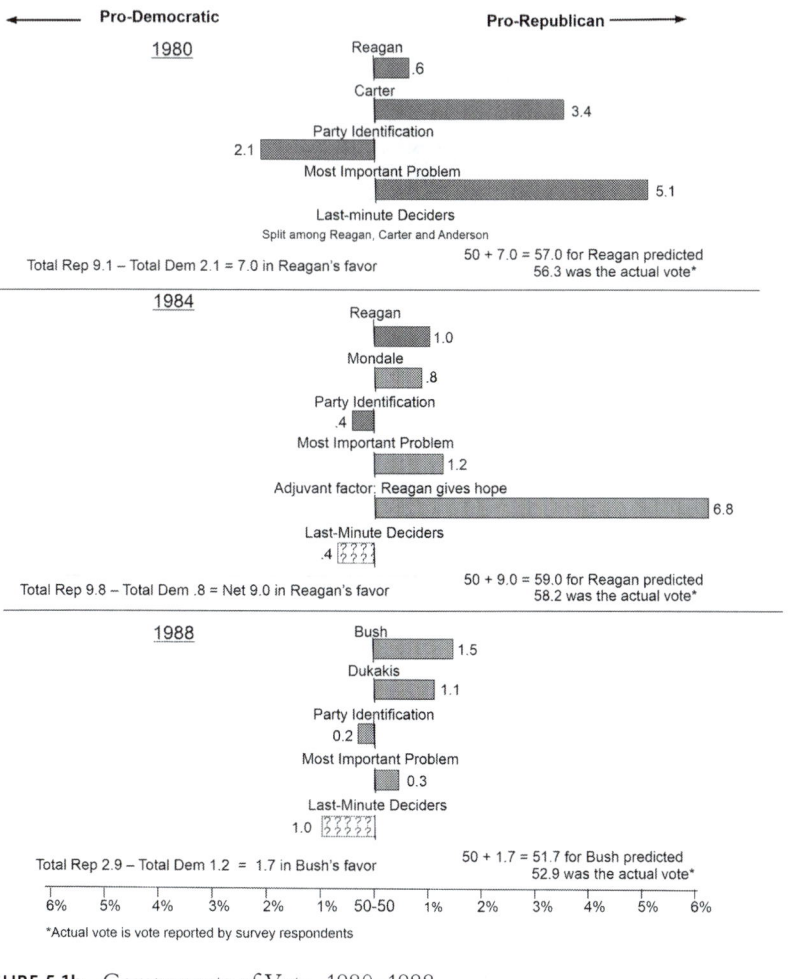

FIGURE 5.1b Components of Vote, 1980–1988.

bars that were unfavorable to that candidate were subtracted, and finally, the effect of the last-minute deciders was added in. This algebraic total of the components shows the extent to which voters, in aggregate, were moved in one or the other partisan direction. It is the distance from the 50–50 point, the point at which there is no overall movement in one partisan direction or the other. This algebraic total is then matched with the actual vote.[2] This comparison is shown at the bottom right side of each year's presentation of the components.

To explain further, let us look, for example, at the numbers at the bottom of 1976 election. Adding up the bars going in the Democratic direction we get 1.6 (Carter) + 1.1 (PID) + 2.8 (MIP) and 0.4 (last-minute deciders) for a total of 5.9. Two bars were in the Republican's favor; that is, 1.1 (Ford) and 3.5 (adjuvant factor) for a total of 4.6 in the Republican direction. The net effect was 5.9 − 4.6 = +1.3.

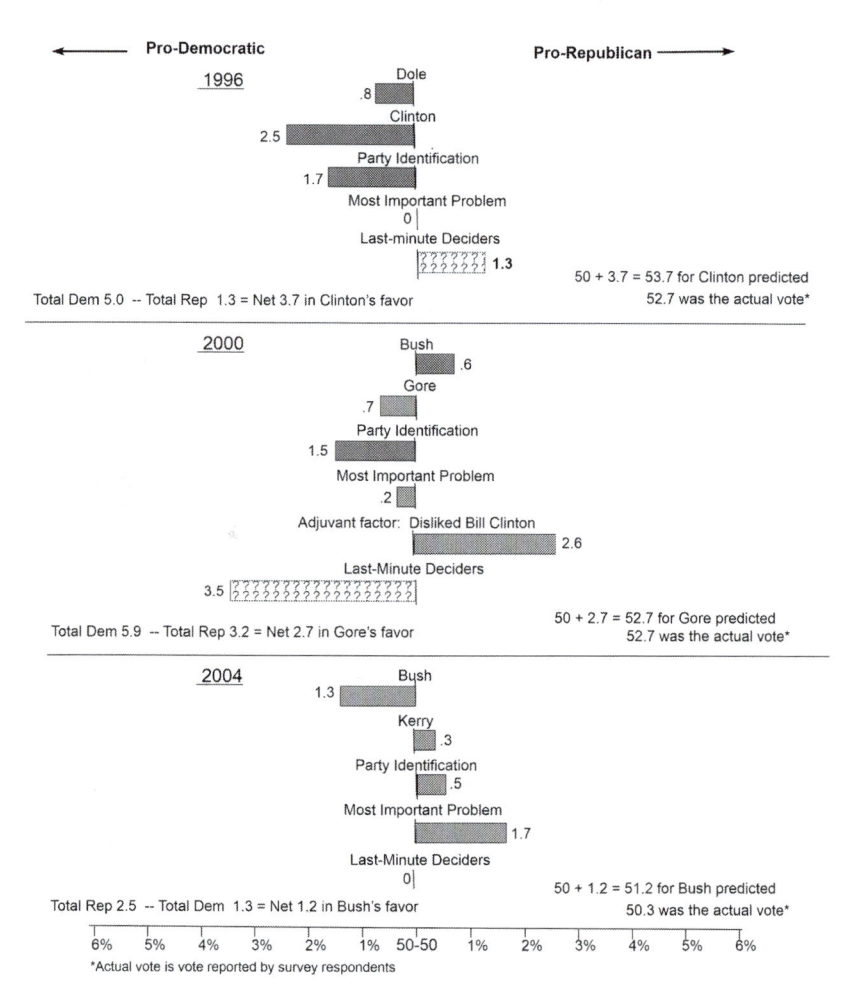

FIGURE 5.1c   Components of Vote, 1996–2004.

Since the Model Equation shows the distance (one way or the other) from 50–50, the +1.3 is added to 50 and thus the estimated election result is 50 + 1.3 = 51.3% for Carter. The actual vote reported by the respondents was 51.1%.

In every election studied the difference between predicted and actual vote is negligible— less than 1 percent. This is a truly remarkable degree of accuracy, especially using open-ended questions. *The theory and methods used in this book are thoroughly validated.*

Each election is entirely different. Sometimes party identification is a major factor, and sometimes it is the MIP that moved voters a lot; in other elections, it is candidates; sometimes it is the late-deciders; and sometimes it is the adjuvant factor. All components contribute, but the amount they contribute varies from election to election.

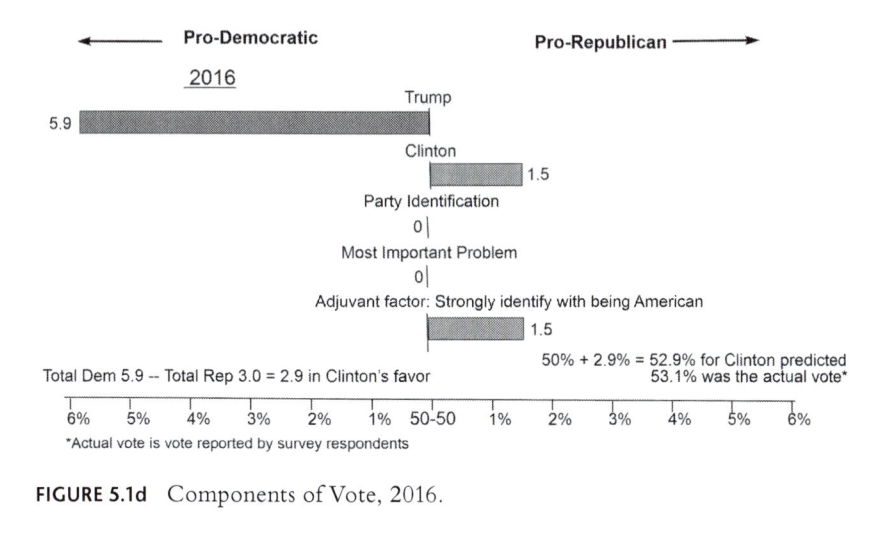

FIGURE 5.1d Components of Vote, 2016.

One may ask why the results found by using the Model Equation in the Introduction are so different from those in this chapter. In the Introduction, we found that in all elections, attitude toward the candidates was the most important factor in voters decision making. In this chapter, candidate components were often quite small. This is because the question we were trying to answer in the Introduction was "how important is each factor in voters' decision making; that is, how much did it weigh?" In this chapter we are looking at the *net* effects. For example, *after weighing each candidate*, a respondent may have both positive and negative attitudes. This would produce a very small *net* effect of the candidate factor.

A Summary of the Components of Each Election

1960: Nixon was viewed very favorably in 1960 as seen in his sizable component. JFK had a small component, mainly because of negative reaction to his being Catholic. JFK was helped a great deal by late-minute deciders.

1964: The very large negative force against Goldwater plus the very positive attitude toward Johnson created a landslide. Johnson's positions on the issues of civil rights and Medicare also helped.

1976: Ford's pardon of Nixon was an adjuvant factor that gave him quite a boost and; as a result, he almost won the election. Apparently, a lot of voters were subconsciously relieved that the Nixon trauma had been put to an end. But there was a very large Issue Public concerned with the economy—both inflation and unemployment—and the Democrats were seen a best able to deal with it.

1980: Carter was so unpopular the he was a large force in the Republican direction. Inflation was rampant and the Democrats (Carter) were no longer seen as able to handle the economy. There was also the problem of hostages being held in Iran. Reagan had almost no net favorability; it was Carter that gave him his victory.

1984: Attitudes toward Reagan were mixed, with almost as many negative as positive, yet he won by a landslide. This is because of the powerful effect of the adjuvant factor—hope. Recall that Reagan often spoke of America as being a "shining city on a hill" and he produced an ad showing "Morning in America." He gave people hope. We saw that Reagan's vote strength was not due to his conservatism, in fact almost no one used the word "conservative" to describe him.

1988: There were no major forces at play. An Issue Public of almost 50 percent had formed because of worry about the national debt (which had been run up under Reagan). But that concern did not translate into unfavorability toward Reagan's successor (H. W. Bush).

1996: This was a lackluster election with no major components. It had the lowest turnout of all elections studied in this book. The mild favorability of Clinton and support from Democratic Party identifiers were enough to get him re-elected.

2000: The 2000 election was lackluster with just two major factors—late-deciders and the adjuvant factor, which was dislike of Clinton. (Gore had been Clinton's vice-president.) With almost no net movement from short-term forces, the result was a tie. (This was the election where the Florida Electoral Vote would determine the winner and the vote in Florida was so close it had to be recounted—a process that took weeks.)

2004: Another lackluster election. By far the major problems in 2004 were the Iraq War and terrorism. There was a lot of dislike of Bush for the Iraq War, but Bush was thought to be a strong leader able to deal with terrorism and prevent another 9/11 type of attack.

2016: Trump was despised[3] by a great many people as seen in his profile in Chapter 4. Sixty-one percent had negative attitudes toward him. This was a component in Hillary Clinton's favor. Yet he won. He was helped by the fact that Hillary Clinton had negative favorability—not nearly as much as Trump's but enough to produce a component in Trump's direction. He did help himself a bit; his slogan "Make America Great Again" resonated with those who strongly identified as being an American (see adjuvant factor). He was also helped by the vagaries of the Electoral College.

Notes

1 I did not create or invent this "*a*" variable. It is an integral part of every regression equation. I simply found out, through trial and error, what variable it represented.
2 The vote reported by the respondent.
3 I use the term "despised" advisedly. I saw all the verbatim like-dislike comments made about Trump and the negative responses were full of emotion and even fear.

6
IDEOLOGY

In the previous chapters, vote was *completely* and very accurately explained by five variables—attitudes toward the Republican and Democratic candidates, party identification, issue concerns, and, occasionally, an adjuvant factor. Ideology did not figure in. When a measure of ideology was entered into the Model Equation in the Introduction, the beta weight was insignificant. When respondents talked about their likes and dislikes of candidates, only rarely was "liberal" or "conservative" mentioned and, when it was, only about five percent mentioned it.

Yet, in the discourse and writings of the political elite, ideology is a primary topic. There is a tendency to place candidates on a liberal-conservative spectrum and speculate whether or not a candidate is too liberal or too conservative. Election returns are characterized as either a movement to the right or the left. Why did ideology not show up as one of the major factors in voters' decisions? In this chapter, I will show that ideology is a background factor that influences voters' evaluations of candidates and issue concerns. These evaluations and issue concerns then become the *proximate* reasons the voter came to his/her decision. This book has been about these proximate influences and therefore, up to now, did not include a factor one-step removed from the final decision—ideology.

In order to study ideology, we need a good measure. The usual way ideology is measured by the political elite is to ask respondents to place themselves on a scale running from very liberal, through middle-of-road to very conservative. This scale is based on the traditional assumption that the ideological distribution of the electorate looks like this—a normal curve with most people in the middle (Figure 6.1).

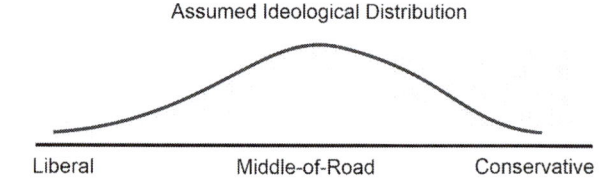

FIGURE 6.1   Assumed Ideological Distribution.

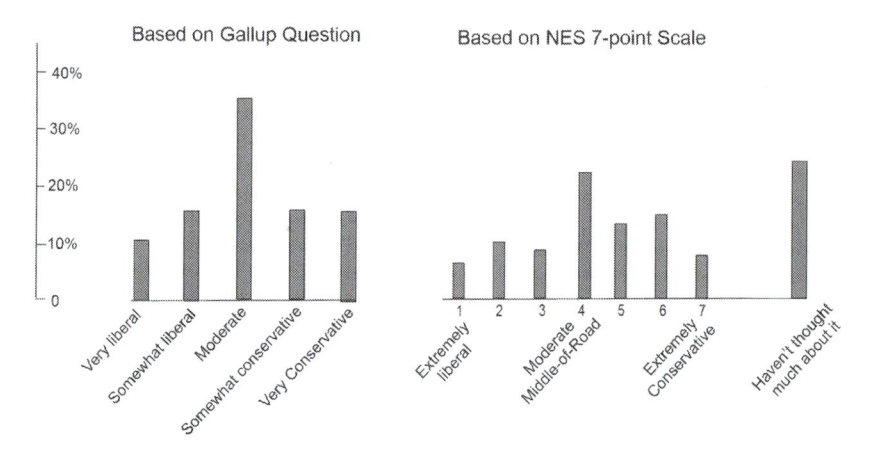

FIGURE 6.2   Ideological Distribution Using Self-placement.

There are different versions of the scale question. Gallup, for example, uses "How would you describe your political views; very conservative, conservative, moderate, liberal, or very liberal?" The ANES uses the following question:

> We hear a lot of talk these days about liberal and conservatives. Here is a seven-point scale on which the political views that people might hold are arranged from extremely liberal to extremely conservative. Where would you place yourself on this scale, or haven't you thought much about this?

The results of asking these questions is shown in Figure 6.2.

Figure 6.2 would seem to confirm the generally accepted assumption about distribution of liberals and conservatives—a normal curve. The problem is that these self-placement questions are highly unreliable and lead to erroneous conclusions.

To check the reliability of a question, one asks the question to the same respondents at two points of time and checks to see if most respondents give the same answer twice. When the ANES question was asked of the same respondents in interviews one or two months apart, *at least half* did not give the same answer twice. Ideology is a very long-term attitude and certainly would not change much in a month or two. It was clear that a great many respondents were guessing. Most of them "flip-flopped" from placing themselves in a position on the 7-point scale in the first interview and then saying they had not thought much about it in the second interview or vice versa. It is well known among pollsters that many respondents who really have no opinion do not want to appear ignorant so they give an answer anyway—usually the middle position, an answer that is non-committal. Note that given the opportunity to admit they do not know, as the ANES version does, there are many fewer in the middle.

The 1988 ANES included the question: "People have different things in mind when they say that someone's political views are liberal or conservative. What sorts of things do you have in mind when you say someone's political views are liberal/conservative?" Of those who had placed themselves on the liberal side of the 7-point scale, almost 25 percent had no idea what "liberal" meant. Of those who had placed themselves on the conservative side, 20 percent had no idea. An additional 7 percent of liberals and 7 percent of conservatives defined these ideological concepts only in terms of personality, not political beliefs. These respondents described "liberals," variously, as people who were rash, impetuous, irresponsible, or as people who were open-minded, fair, compassionate, do-gooders. Conservatives were thought to be cautious, careful, and decisive, or alternatively, as closed-minded, self-centered, and intolerant. Furthermore, 17 percent of liberals and 11 percent of conservatives gave only vague, overly generalized answers. *All told, 48 percent of self-placed liberals and 38 percent of self-placed conservatives had little or no idea of what it meant to be what they were calling themselves.*

There needed to be a way to screen out these guessers and I found one. I used four questions in the ANES surveys that explicitly sought information about attitudes toward liberals and conservatives. If respondents answer consistently and knowledgably across these four questions, it was highly likely that they were not guessing their way through and were real ideologues. The four questions were: the 7-point self-placement scale (quoted above), two thermometer questions that asked respondents' feelings (warm or cold) toward "liberals" and "conservatives," and a question which asked: "Would you say that one of the parties is more conservative than the other at the national level? Which party is more conservative?" Since my measure of ideology is based on Placement on the liberal-conservative scale, Thermometer questions and a Recognition of which party is conservative, I refer to it as the PTR measure.

Those who began the series of questions by placing themselves on the conservative side of the 7-point scale would be expected to be warm or hot toward conservatives, a feeling the was measured by the conservative thermometer. These conservatives would also be expected to be cool or cold toward liberals. Similarly, liberals would be expected to be warm or hot toward liberals and cold toward conservatives. Respondents were given a final test; did they know that the Republican Party is the conservative party? Anyone who cleared these

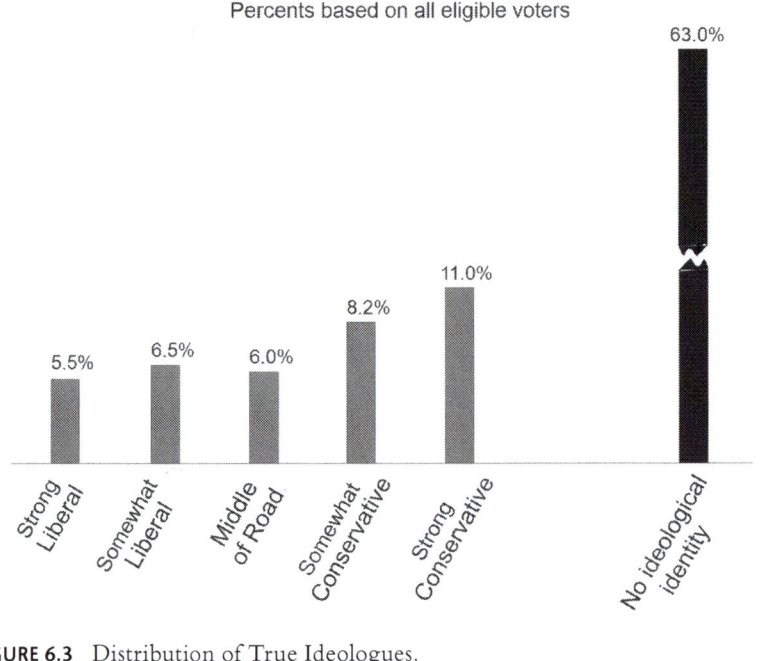

Percents based on all eligible voters

FIGURE 6.3 Distribution of True Ideologues.

four hurdles were considered to be a *true* conservative or a *true* liberal. Middle-of-the-roaders were consistently in the middle of all scales and never answered "don't know."

Figure 6.3 shows the distribution of *true* ideologues along with the non-ideologues. (Non-ideologues are those who did not clear the four hurdles.) Since there was little variation from year to year, data in Figure 6.3 was averaged over the 2004, 2008, 2012, and 2016 election studies. *The distribution is not a normal curve and there is almost no one in the middle.*[1]

The fact that 50 to 60 percent of the public cannot accurately identify themselves as liberals or conservatives should not be interpreted as evidence of an ignorant and incompetent electorate. As we will see momentarily, most of the public have belief systems. What we have looked at so far regarding ideologues is simply labeling. One can have a belief system but not know that it has a "liberal" or "conservative" label. The concepts of "liberal" and "conservative," after all, were invented in academia and most often used in the commentary of the political elite. But unless the average citizen spends lot of time listening to media commentators or reading about electoral politics, how can they be expected to become familiar with the terms? These concepts are rarely taught in schools.

Let me make an analogy with the jargon of sportscasters. Let us say that someone is not an avid fan of football and does not watch a lot of games and thus does not become familiar with the jargon of sportscasters, yet does watch the big game—the Superbowl. Let us say that while watching the Superbowl someone hears the sportscaster say, "They're in a nickel defense; now they are blitzing" or "There is a screen pass to the tight end." The watcher would not know what these terms meant yet could see which team was better and had the most effective leader (quarterback). Similarly, an average citizen, who does not watch a lot of political commentary and thus learn the jargon, is nonetheless likely to participate in the "big game" (the presidential election). He or she can observe the performance of the candidates and decide who would be the best leader and how well a party (a team) was doing without knowing the jargon of politics.

Belief Systems

If we want to know a voter's ideology, we need to know much more than just a label, we need to know what voters believe and what they value. Ideologies consist of several beliefs and values that have come together in peoples' minds to form a belief system. It would seem obvious that one would use questions that measure beliefs and values to find belief systems. However, almost all political science studies of ideology over the past sixty years have not used these measures; rather they have used opinions on contemporary issues as indicators of belief systems. Issues come and go, and opinions about ongoing issues often change rapidly. By definition, beliefs and values are long term and usually never change once they are formed early in life. Belief systems effect one's opinion about contemporary issues, not the other way around.

My definition of a belief system is simply "a set of beliefs that the individual has brought together." I do not require the constraints that most researchers have often imposed, such as interrelatedness.

I recently found a way to measure belief systems. First, I looked through all the ANES studies in search of questions that measured beliefs or values.[2] Only four studies—1992, 2004, 2012, and 2016—contained enough of these questions to measure complete sets of beliefs and values. I found about 40 belief or value questions in each of these four studies. Each question allowed the respondent two choices—a choice in one direction and a polar opposite choice.

It was then necessary to find which of these 40 questions voters included in their belief systems. Taking this bunch of questions, I then let respondents themselves reveal their belief systems by looking for patterns of responses. I had no idea what beliefs people would bring together. I used a computer program to find *sets* of questions a significant number of respondents had answered *consistently* in one ideological direction. Two separate sets of questions—the same questions in each set—emerged in each of the four ANES studies. Each set contained at least eleven questions. These repeated findings with the same result give strong evidence that the method is reliable. The items in these sets are shown in Lists 1 and 2. (See Appendix C for details of this method of finding sets.)

List 1: The Liberal Dimension

The Liberal response is indicated by putting it in capital letters and labeling it L
Opposite to Liberal response is in non-capitalized letters and labeled OL

Strong, Active Government

1. L   "WE NEED A STRONG GOVERNMENT TO HANDLE TODAY'S COMPLEX ECONOMIC PROBLEMS;

1. OL. or, the free market can handle these problems without government being involved."

2. OL. "The less government, the better; or,

2. L.   THERE ARE MORE THINGS THAT GOVERNMENT SHOULD BE DOING."

3. OL. "The main reason government has become bigger over the years is because it has gotten involved in things that people should do for themselves; or,

3. L.   GOVERNMENT HAS BECOME BIGGER BECAUSE THE PROBLEMS WE FACE HAVE BECOME BIGGER."

Egalitarian

4. L.   "A big problem is not giving everyone an equal chance." (AGREE)

Willingness to Spend for Services and To Help Others (Altruism)

5. L.   "SOME PEOPLE FEEL THE GOVERNMENT IN WASHINGTON SHOULD SEE TO IT THAT EVERY PERSON HAS A JOB AND A GOOD STANDARD OF LIVING.

5. OL. Others think the government should just let each person get ahead on their own."

6. L.   "GOVERNMENT SHOULD MAKE EVERY EFFORT TO IMPROVE THE SOCIAL AND ECONOMIC POSITION OF BLACKS AND OTHER MINORITIES

6. OL   government should not make special effort to help minorities because they should help themselves."

7. OL. "Some people think the government should provide fewer services even in areas such as health and education in order to reduce spending.

7. L.   OTHER PEOPLE FEEL IT IS IMPORTANT FOR THE GOVERNMENT TO PROVIDE MANY MORE SERVICES EVEN IF IT MEANS AN INCREASE IN SPENDING."

"I am going to read you a list of federal programs. For each one, I would like you to tell me whether you would like to see spending INCREASED or decreased"

8. L.   PUBLIC SCHOOLS
9. L.   WELFARE PROGRAMS
10. L. CHILD CARE
11. L. AID TO THE POOR

List 2: The Conservative Dimension

The Conservative response is indicated by putting it in capital letters and labeling it C
Opposite to Conservative response is in non-capitalized letters and labeled OC

Strong Military and Defense

1. OC. "Some people believe that we should spend much less money for defense.

1. C Others feel that DEFENSE SPENDING SHOULD BE GREATLY INCREASED."

2. C. "How important is it for the U.S. to have a strong military force in order to be effective in dealing with our enemies?" (EXTREMELY IMPORTANT)

Religious Beliefs

3. C. "Do you consider RELIGION TO BE AN IMPORTANT PART OF YOUR LIFE

3. OC or not?"

4. C. "THE BIBLE IS THE ACTUAL WORD OF GOD TO BE TAKEN LITERALLY, WORD FOR WORD"

Patriotism

5. C. "When you see the American flag flying does it make you feel EXTREMELY GOOD,"

5. OC. very good, or not very good

6. C. "How strong is your love for your country?" (EXTREMELY STRONG)

6. OC. somewhat strong, not very strong

7. C. "Is being an American EXTREMELY IMPORTANT to you personally?"

7. OC. somewhat important, not too important

Moral Lifestyle

8. C. "The newer lifestyles are contributing to the breakdown of our society." (AGREE)

9. C. "The country would have fewer problems if there were more emphasis on traditional family ties." (AGREE)

10. C. "Do you think gay or lesbian couples, in other words, homosexual couples, should be legally permitted to adopt children?" (NO)

11. OC. "Should same-sex couples be allowed to marry,

11. C. or do YOU THINK THEY SHOULD NOT BE ALLOWED TO MARRY?"

List 1 contains the set of items that were most frequently chosen from among all forty items. They are items that are customarily considered liberal beliefs. They are shown in capital letters and labeled "L." I call this set the Liberal Dimension. A second set of items was also discovered as explained in Appendix C. These items were also frequently chosen and measure beliefs that are customarily considered conservative. They are shown in capital letters in List 2 and labeled "C." I call this set the Conservative Dimension. Some individuals took positions that were the *polar opposite* of the preponderant one. These items are shown in non-capitalized letters and labeled with an "O" for opposite.

Within each set of questions, there were subsets of like items. The liberal set (Liberal Dimension) had subsets that measured "Strong, Active Government," "Egalitarianism," and "Willingness to Spend on Services and to Help Others (Altruism)." The conservative set (Conservative Dimension) had "Strong Military and Defense," "Religious Beliefs," "Patriotism," and "Moral Lifestyle." To be clear, the Liberal belief system is made up of all or almost all of the eleven liberal items, and the Conservative belief system is made up of all or almost all of the eleven conservative items. The subsets simply group like items together to allow for parsimonious interpretation.

Wording of questions was extremely important. Some of the ANES questions that were designed to measure a certain belief failed to do so. The wording did not reflect the respondents' belief. For example, there were six questions that attempted to register belief in equality. Only one was expressed in a way that resonated with respondents and thus was identified as one belonging to their set of beliefs. Four questions were asked about moral traditionalism, only two reflected how respondents thought about this and thus fit into their belief system.

Some of the subsets of a belief system are measured by four questions (such as willingness to spend), some by three questions (such as patriotism and role of government), some by two (such as religious beliefs) and another by just one question (egalitarianism). The number of items that make up a subset of beliefs has nothing to do with the importance of the subset in the belief system. The number of items in a subset is depended on whether or not the ANES principle investigators had framed a question in a way that reflected one of the beliefs in the respondent's belief system.

Having identified *sets of questions* that showed up because enough individuals had answered them consistently in one ideological direction, a key step in the analysis was to find which *individuals* had answered in this consistent fashion. Each individual was given a score that measured how many questions they answered in a certain direction. Some had given the liberal answer to all eleven, or nearly all eleven, questions in the liberal set and thus were named "Liberals." Some others had taken the polar opposite positions on the liberal set. These were labeled "Polar Conservatives." And some had answered randomly and thus were not part of that dimension. Similarly, those who answered all or most all of the questions in the conservative set in the conservative direction were named "Conservatives," and those who took the polar opposite positions on the Conservative Dimension were labeled "Polar Liberal." Again, random response indicated No Belief System on that dimension.

Beliefs Not Associated with Any Dimension

Several items that are commonly thought of as hallmarks in the liturgy of conservative beliefs—abortion, the death penalty, no gun control, the role of women, and spending on Social Security—did not show up in the conservative set. A question on regulation of business was asked in 2012, but could not be used because it had only been asked once, and spending on foreign aid (which was only asked about in 2004) did not show up at all in the conservative belief system that year. Civil liberties questions concerning torture and warrantless wiretapping, asked in 2012, did not have a significant showing on either the Liberal or the Conservative Dimensions.

A question regarding income inequality was asked in the 2012 ANES: "Do you favor, oppose or neither favor or oppose the government trying to make income differences smaller?" This item was part of the Liberal Dimension that year, but was not used in this study since it would make the dimension incomparable with the 1992, 2004, and 2016 dimensions when the question was not asked.

Figure 6.4a shows graphically the proportions of respondents identified as Liberals and Polar Conservatives in each of the years studied. Figure 6.4b shows the proportions of Conservatives and Polar Liberals.

The proportion of Liberals has remained quite constant—at about 50 percent—throughout the last twenty-five years. Polar Liberals—those who

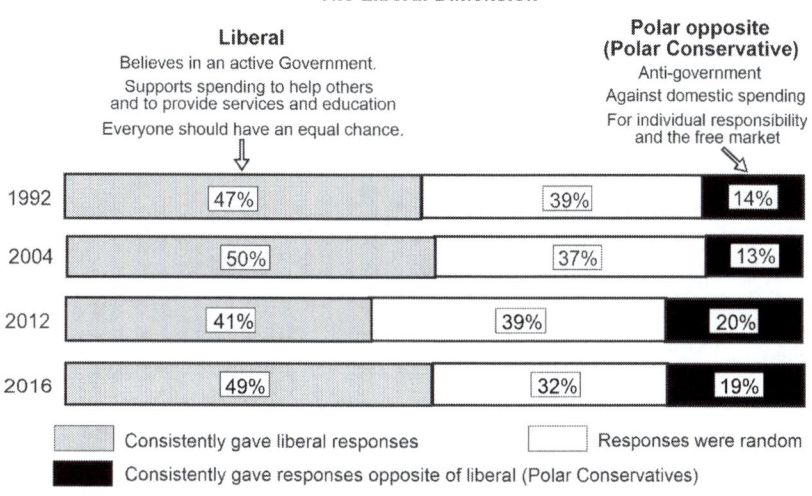

FIGURE 6.4a Distribution of Electorate on the Liberal Dimension.

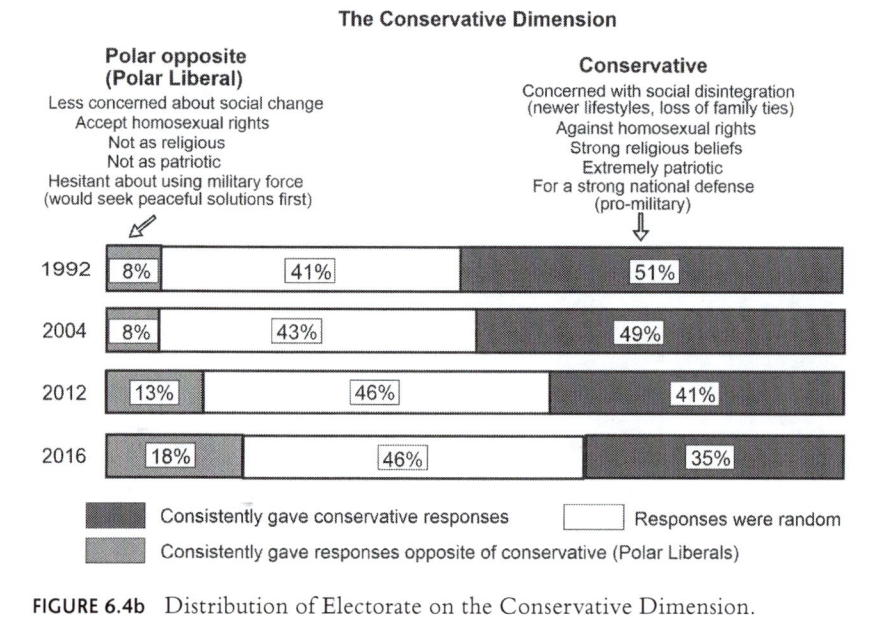

The Conservative Dimension

Polar opposite (Polar Liberal)	Conservative
Less concerned about social change	Concerned with social disintegration (newer lifestyles, loss of family ties)
Accept homosexual rights	Against homosexual rights
Not as religious	Strong religious beliefs
Not as patriotic	Extremely patriotic
Hesitant about using military force (would seek peaceful solutions first)	For a strong national defense (pro-military)

1992 8% 41% 51%

2004 8% 43% 49%

2012 13% 46% 41%

2016 18% 46% 35%

■ Consistently gave conservative responses ☐ Responses were random

■ Consistently gave responses opposite of conservative (Polar Liberals)

FIGURE 6.4b   Distribution of Electorate on the Conservative Dimension.

were the opposite of conservatives—went from 8 to 18 percent. Conservatives declined from an average of 54 percent in 1992 and 2004 to about 38 percent in 2012 and 2016. An average of only about 15 percent are Polar Conservatives. They are ones who are anti-government and against domestic spending. On net, Figure 6.1 shows a slight shift toward liberalism.

Combining Sets of Beliefs

Analytically, two sets of beliefs have been discovered, but they are *not held separately* in peoples' minds. They merge together into one overall belief system. *Every respondent is somewhere on both the* LIBERAL DIMENSION *and on the* CONSERVATIVE DIMENSION. Someone may be liberal on the LIBERAL DIMENSION and have a random response pattern on the CONSERVATIVE DIMENSION; or be a liberal on the LIBERAL DIMENSION and be a Polar Liberal on the CONSERVATIVE DIMENSION, or a Conservative on the CONSERVATIVE DIMENSION and have a random response pattern on the LIBERAL DIMENSION, and so forth. There are nine possible combinations of the two dimensions, or nine possible blocs of belief systems (Figure 6.5, Matrix).

In the Matrix, we can see all nine of the combinations that are possible when we merge the LIBERAL DIMENSION and on the CONSERVATIVE DIMENSION. The merging is done by simply cross tabulating the two dimensions.

In the center of the top row of the Matrix, we see those who were conservative on the CONSERVATIVE DIMENSION and had random responses on the LIBERAL

Matrix
Combining Liberal and Conservative Dimensions

Liberal Dimension (from Figure 6.4a)

<table>
<tr><td rowspan="6" style="writing-mode:vertical">Conservative Dimension (from Figure 6.4b)</td><td></td><td>Liberal</td><td>Not on Dimension</td><td>Polar Conservative</td></tr>
<tr><td>Conservative</td><td>Bi-ideological

Active government   Moral Life styles
Spending to help others   Religious
Gov't services, education   Patriotism
Equality   Strong Military</td><td>Ordinary Conservative

Moral Life styles
Religious
Patriotism
Strong Military</td><td>Strong Conservative

Moral Life styles   Anti-government
Religious   Anti-domestic spending
Patriotism   Individual responsibility
Strong Military   Free market economy</td></tr>
<tr><td>Not on Dimension</td><td>Ordinary Liberal

Active government
Spending to help others
Gov't services, education
Equality</td><td>No belief system</td><td>Polar Conservative

Anti-government
Anti-domestic spending
Individual responsibility
Free market economy</td></tr>
<tr><td>Polar Liberal</td><td>Strong Liberal

Active government   Tolerant
Spending to help others   For gay rights
Gov't services, education   Not religious
Equality   Less patriotic
Use diplomacy
not military force</td><td>Polar Liberal

Tolerant
For gay rights
Not religious
Less patriotic
Use diplomacy
not military force</td><td>None</td></tr>
</table>

FIGURE 6.5 Ideological Blocs Matrix.

DIMENSION. These are labeled "Ordinary Conservatives." In the center left cell are those who were liberal on the LIBERAL DIMENSION but did not show up on the CONSERVATIVE DIMENSION (responded randomly). These are labeled "Ordinary Liberals." *The beliefs of Ordinary Conservatives and Ordinary Liberals are not diametrically opposite of each other, just different.*

The Strong Liberals have the belief systems of the Ordinary Liberals and, in addition, they are Polar Liberals. Similarly, Strong Conservatives have the belief system of Ordinary Conservatives and, in addition, are Polar Conservatives. They have a double set of beliefs—each composed of several components. This large set of beliefs make them true believers who can be expected to be very rigid and likely to apply their belief system when evaluating candidates.

The upper left cell represents someone who is both liberal and conservative. This would seem logically and psychologically impossible, yet if we look at the substance of the beliefs held by both Ordinary Liberals and Ordinary Conservatives, we can see how these two belief systems could be held by the same person. For example, it is perfectly possible for someone to believe in equality and believe that we should have an active government that can do good things (such as fund schools, child care, and help the poor), yet at the same time be patriotic, want a strong national defense and be concerned with the moral breakdown in society. In fact, many Americans have both a liberal and a conservative belief system simultaneously and apparently are not conflicted. They are Bi-ideological.

However, it would not be possible for someone to be both a Polar Liberal and a Polar Conservative since they would have diametrically opposing beliefs. Indeed, no one showed up with this combination of beliefs.

Some are polar ideologues only. The Polar Conservatives have beliefs that are the polar opposites of Liberals on the LIBERAL DIMENSION but have random beliefs on the CONSERVATIVE DIMENSION. Polar Liberals are those who have beliefs which are the polar opposite of conservatives on the CONSERVATIVE DIMENSION but have random beliefs on the LIBERAL DIMENSION. These blocs were too small to be reliably analyzed, so they will seldom appear in future tables.

Finally, some among the electorate have neither a liberal or a conservative belief system and are labeled "No Belief System."

The Blocs

The proportions of the electorate who were in each of the ideological blocs are shown in Figure 6.6. *This is what the ideological composition of the electorate looks like.* The percentages in the figure are based on the entire potential electorate.

The blocs should not be considered as arrayed along a single continuum from left to right. *Rather, they consist of seven separate blocs, each with its own distinct set of beliefs and also a bloc with no belief system.* It should not come as a surprise that in a society as large and diverse as ours that there are several different belief systems, not just one overall left–right system.

We see in Figure 6.6 that the blocs have remained similar in size year after year from 1992 to 2016. There was some change during this period, but not a lot in all that time. Polar Conservatives and Strong Conservatives (combined) grew 8 percentage points in twenty-four years, while Ordinary Conservatives decreased by about 9 percentage points. Polar Liberals and Strong Liberals (combined) increased by 12 percentage points while Ordinary Liberals remained the same. Bi-ideologicals decreased by 8 percentage points.

Those blocs on the left side of Figure 6.6 are polarized. *The bulk of the electorate are on the right side—in blocs that do not have opposing beliefs.* The total proportion of the electorate that was ideologically polarized (Strong Liberals, Polar Liberals, Strong Conservatives, and Polar Conservatives) increased by 20 percentage points in the twenty-four years between 1992 and 2016 (about 0.85 percent a year). Although this was a noticeable increase, this ideologically *polarized portion of the electorate still amounts to less that half—40 percent.*

(See Appendix D for the demographic composition of the blocs.)

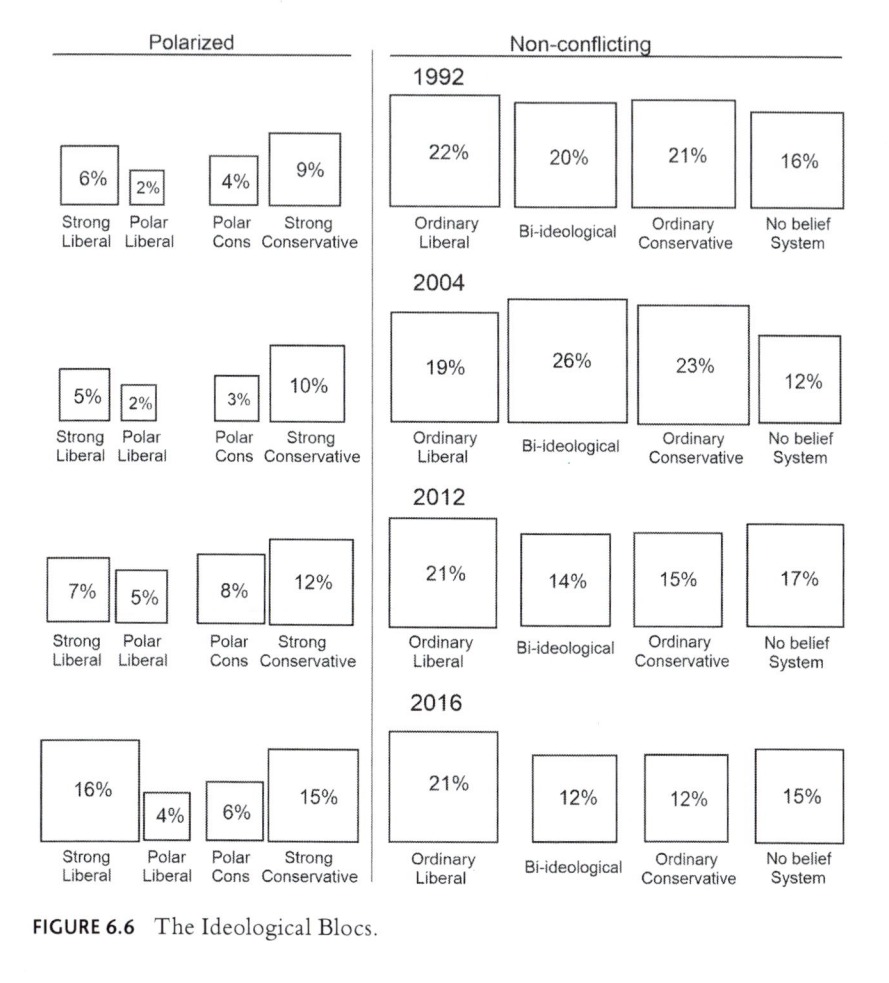

FIGURE 6.6 The Ideological Blocs.

Validation of My Measure of Belief Systems

Ideology has two manifestations: a belief system and an identification. Earlier, I used my PTR measure to find those who *truly* identify with an ideology. The validity of my method of finding the ideological belief systems (blocs) can be found by comparing the blocs with the true identifiers; by seeing if those with liberal belief systems identify as liberals and those with conservative belief systems identify as conservatives. Table 6.1, which cross-tabulates the two measures, shows a remarkable degree of validity. *In only twenty-nine cases among the 4,170 examined, was there a mismatch between belief system and ideological identity.*

Furthermore, we would hypothesize that Strong Liberals and Strong Conservatives would be more likely to realize that they are liberals or conservatives. The soundness of my method is shown by the fact that the Strong Liberals and Strong Conservatives were highly likely to identify as liberals or

TABLE 6.1 Validation: Comparing Belief Systems with Ideological Identification Average of 2004, 2012, and 2016 Data

	True Ideological Identity from PTR Measure						
	Very Liberal	Liberal	Middle-of-Road	Conserv	Very Conserv	No Identity	
Strong Liberal	46%	22	★	0	0	30	100%
Strong Conservative	0%	0	0	16	62	21	100%
Ordinary Liberal	9%	11	8	★	0	72	100%
Ordinary Conservative	★	★	6	14	15	65	100%

★ Less than 2 percent.

conservatives respectively, but only about 30 percent of weaker ideologues—the Ordinary Liberals and Ordinary Conservatives—knew that their beliefs had a label. Finally, we would expect the Bi-ideologicals would find it difficult to place themselves on a dimension that had two *opposing* poles—liberal OR conservative. Indeed, 84 percent of them were in the No Identity category.

The Effect of Ideology on Issue Concerns

At the beginning of this chapter, I hypothesized that ideology influences issue concerns and attitudes toward candidates. Now that we have a measure of ideology, let us test the hypothesis by using the Issue Publics tables of Chapter 3, Table 3.2. The beliefs of conservatives would predispose them to be concerned with moral lifestyles and a strong military. And indeed, the moral decay of the country was a major concern of conservatives in 1988, 1992, 1996, and 2000. In the Cold War period from 1960 to 1988,[3] military spending and relations with USSR were often cited as the most important problem by conservatives. Conservatives also were troubled by the national debt. Liberals were concerned with the poor, problems of the aged, equality for blacks, education, and medical care—a clear reflection of their beliefs.

Ideological Influence on Attitudes toward Candidates

Table 6.2 shows a definite influence of *strong* ideology on attitudes toward candidates. Strong and Polar Republicans almost always have a lot to say in favor of their candidate, and nothing to say against. Strong and Polar Liberals do the same. The only exceptions were numerous negative comments about H. W. Bush in 1992, and Donald Trump in 2016 made by Strong and Polar Conservatives, and numerous negative comments about Bill Clinton in 1992 and Hillary Clinton in 2016 made by Strong and Polar Liberals.

TABLE 6.2 Effect of Ideology on Attitudes toward Candidates

	Strong Conservatives Polar Conservatives				Strong Liberals Polar Liberals				Weak Republicans, Weak Democrats Bi-ideological, No Belief System			
1992	Pro Bush[a]	Anti Bush	Pro Clinton[b]	Anti Clinton	Pro Bush[a]	Anti Bush	Pro Clinton[b]	Anti Clinton	Pro Bush[a]	Anti Bush	Pro Clinton[b]	Anti Clinton
None	16%	36%	68%	13%	70%	8%	14%	52%	54%	34%	42%	54%
1 remark	16	22	13	19	15	11	9	24	15	18	16	22
>1 remarks	68	42	19	68	15	81	77	24	31	48	42	24
Total	100%	100%	100%	100%	100%	100%	100%	100%	100%	100%	100%	100%
N	297	297	297	297	170	170	170	170	1783	1783	1783	1783
2004	Pro Bush[c]	Anti Bush	Pro Kerry	Anti Kerry	Pro Bush[c]	Anti Bush	Pro Kerry	Anti Kerry	Pro Bush[c]	Anti Bush	Pro Kerry	Anti Kerry
None	8%	61%	79%	11%	86%	3%	21%	61%	52%	40%	52%	54%
1 remark	24	19	10	25	6	20	17	16	17	21	17	19
>1 remarks	68	20	11	64	8	77	62	23	31	39	31	27
Total	100%	100%	100%	100%	100%	100%	100%	100%	100%	100%	100%	100%
N	140	140	140	140	80	80	80	80	843	843	843	843
2016	Pro Trump	Anti Trump	Pro Clinton[d]	Anti Clinton	Pro Trump	Anti Trump	Pro Clinton[d]	Anti Clinton	Pro Trump	Anti Trump	Pro Clinton[d]	Anti Clinton
None	11%	42%	93%	3%	85%	3%	5%	47%	56%	29%	47%	42%
1 remarks	30	33	6	33	10	15	31	32	24	30	24	33
> 1 remarks	59	25	1	64	5	82	64	21	20	41	29	25
Total	100%	100%	100%	100%	100%	100%	100%	100%	100%	100%	100%	100%
N	145	145	145	145	135	135	135	135	404	404	404	404

a George H. W. Bush.
b Bill Clinton.
c W. Bush.
d Hillary Clinton.

TABLE 6.3 Influence of Ideology on Vote

	2004			2012			2016		
	Kerry	*Bush*		*Obama*	*Romney*		*Clinton*	*Trump*	
Strong Liberal	98%	2	100%	98%	2	100%	100%	0	100%
Strong Conservative	1%	99	100%	4%	96	100%	2%	98	100%
Ordinary Conservative	26%	74	100%	31%	69	100%	21%	79	100%
Ordinary Liberal	80%	20	100%	92%	8	100%	84%	16	100%
Bi-ideological	62%	38	100%	69%	31	100%	54%	46	100%
No Belief System	63%	37	100%	61%	39	100%	47%	53	100%

Those with less-strong mind-sets—the Weak Republicans, Weak Democrats, Bi-ideologicals, and those with No Belief System take a more balanced view of candidates; they have a fairly equal number of favorable and unfavorable attitudes. The only exceptions were an unusual amount of negative comments about H. W. Bush and Bill Clinton in 1992 and a very large set of anti-Trump comments in 2016.

Now let us turn to effect of ideology on the partisan direction of the vote. We see in Table 6.3 that close to 100 percent of both Strong Liberals and Strong Conservatives consistently voted for the candidate closest to their ideology. If one knows someone is a strong ideologue, one can predict his or her vote with almost complete certainty. (This is testament to the validity of my method of identifying blocs of belief systems.)

Ordinary ideologues are less strongly influenced by their ideology. Over the years of this study, an average of 18 percent of Ordinary Liberals and 26 percent of Ordinary Conservatives defected and voted for the candidate who did not share their beliefs. For example, 20 percent of Ordinary Liberals voted for McCain in 2004 and 16 percent for Trump in 2016. Twenty-six percent of Ordinary Conservatives voted for Kerry in 2004 and 31 percent for Obama in 2012.

The voting behavior of Bi-ideologicals and those with No Belief System was, as expected, unpredictable.

Notes

1 For years, the Democratic Party has followed a strategy called "The Third Way." It calls for appealing to the middle. There are very few in the middle to appeal to.

2 Beliefs are long-term attitudes that are central in an attitude structure and resist change. They are *general*, neutral (non-polemic), substantive statements that have no specific referent such as a recently passed law or specific policy proposal. Values are important life goals or societal conditions desired by a person. Values are usually broad, abstract concepts like freedom, justice, patriotism, family, piety, morality, altruism, and service to others.

3 The Vietnam War took the place of the Cold War in the list of concerns in 1968 and 1972.

7

POLARIZATION

In this chapter, we are going to examine the extent of polarization in the American electorate. There is no question that Congress is polarized as Figure 7.1 shows. Indeed, Congress is totally polarized and thus paralyzed. It can get almost nothing done.

We see that in the 1970s there was considerable ideological overlap; quite a few Democrats were more conservative than some Republicans and vice versa. By 2011 there was a wide gap with liberal Democrats on one side and conservative Republicans on the other with a gulf in-between. (It should be noted that the measures of ideology used in Figure 7.1 are based on roll-call votes, which reflect the effectiveness of the discipline imposed by party leaders. Many congressmen and senators may privately hold different attitudes.)

Is this great divide in Congress a reflection of a divided electorate?

The Rigid and the Malleable

If we want to understand the extent of political division in the electorate, we must look not only at ideological polarization but at partisan division, as well. It is often assumed that liberals are Democrats and Democrats are liberals; conservatives are Republican and Republicans are conservatives—the terms are often used interchangeably. Yet, this is not the case. Only an average of 58 percent of the Strong Liberals and 48 percent of Ordinary Liberals identify with the Democratic Party. Over 40 percent of these two blocs are Independents. It is only the Strong Conservatives who are party oriented, with an average of 70 percent identifying as Republican. Ordinary Conservatives have mixed party identity; 44 percent of them identify, appropriately, as Republicans but 16 percent think they are Democrats. It is interesting to note that Bi-ideologicals, who one would think would be Independents, are 50 percent Democrats. It is

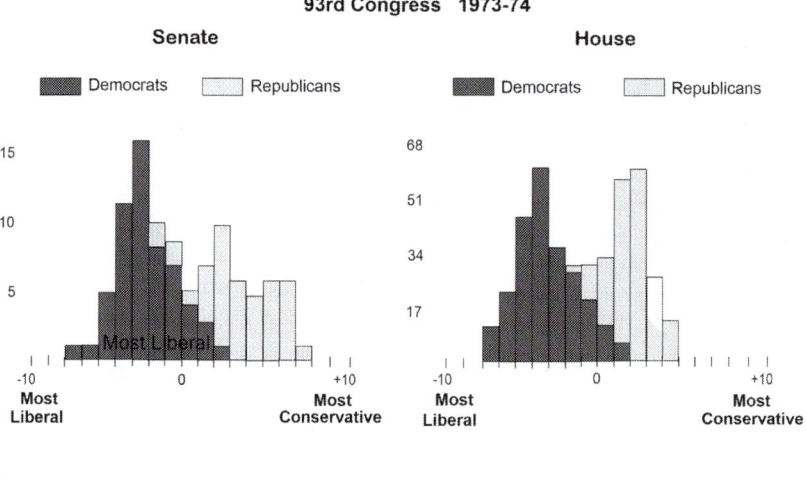

Data is from https://www.pewresearch.org/fact-tank /2014/06/12/polarized-politics-in-congress-began-in-the-1970s-and-has-been-getting-worse-ever-since/

FIGURE 7.1 Ideological Scores of Senators and Congressmen, 1973–74 and 2011–2012.

only those with No Belief System that tend to be Independents (50 percent). In sum, knowing one's belief system does not automatically determine one's party identification and vice versa.

We saw in Figure 2.3 that Strong Republicans and Strong Democrats almost never stray to the other side in an election; they are impervious to short-term forces. The same is true of Strong Conservatives and Strong Liberals—almost every strong ideologue votes for the candidate closest to their ideology (see Table 6.3). Since Strong Conservatives are not necessarily Strong Republicans, we must add these two groups together to find the total number of unmovable Conservatives and Republicans. I will call them the Rigid Right.

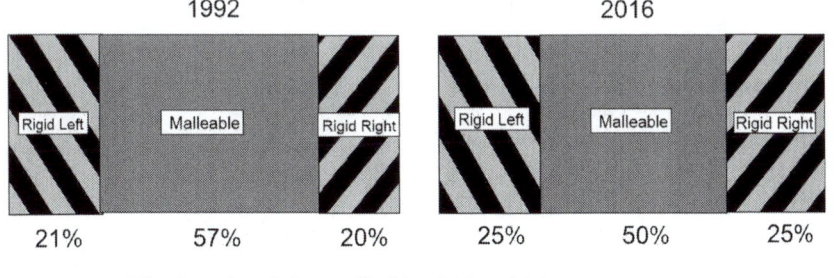

FIGURE 7.2 The Rigid and the Malleable 1992 and 2016.

Likewise, we must add together those who are Strong Liberals or Strong Democrats (or both) to find the unmovable Liberals and Democrats. I will call them the Rigid Left. I found that, as of 2016, 25 percent of the electorate were Rigid Right and 25 percent Rigid Left.

The rest of the electorate I will call "Malleable"; they are the Weak Democrats, Weak Republicans, Independents, Ordinary Liberals, the Ordinary Conservatives, the Bi-Ideologicals, and those with No Belief System[1] They can be persuaded to vote for the other side. *Note that they are not just Independents.* Also, they are not "swing" voters because the word "swing" implies that they constantly go back and forth as on a swing. It takes a special set of short-term forces in a particular election to persuade some of them to move. Also, they should not be called "centrists," which implies they are in the neutral center of the liberal–conservative spectrum. Most of them have a belief system.

The Rigid and the Malleable are not distributed evenly across the country. Urban areas are the most Rigid places, with over half Rigid Left and only a third Malleable. The next most Rigid places are the rural towns with about 40 percent Rigid Right, but these towns are nearly half Malleable. Suburbs are half Malleable with the other half split between Rigid Right and Rigid Left. When change takes place, it is most likely to be in the suburbs.

To demonstrate that my characterization of the electorate produces the predicted effects—that the Rigid are quite unchangeable and the Malleable do change—let us look at the results of recent elections (Table 7.1).

TABLE 7.1 Vote by Rigidity

	2004		*2012*		*2016*	
	Kerry	*Bush*	*Obama*	*Romney*	*Clinton*	*Trump*
Rigid Left	97%	3%	97%	3%	98%	2%
Rigid Right	4%	96%	5%	95%	8%	92%
Malleable	55%	45%	57%	43%	60%	40%

We see that in all elections except one (2016),[2] 95 percent or more of the Rigid voted for the candidate of their political persuasion. The Malleable split their vote.

If we compare Figure 7.1 (division in Congress) with Figure 7.2 (division in the public) we see that the public is only half paralyzed but Congress is totally paralyzed. *Congress reflects only half of the electorate. The other half goes unrepresented.*

The Effect of the Mass Media

One of the first things one notices in looking at Figure 7.2 is that there has been very little change (4 or 5 percent) in the proportions of Rigid Right and Rigid Left in the twenty-four years from 1992 to 2016.[3] (That is 0.2 percent a year each.) Rush Limbaugh, the well-known right-wing radio commentator, began broadcasting nationally in 1988 and the right-wing news channel, Fox News, began in 1996. Yet the proportion of Rigid Right has increased by only 5 percent. At the same time, the Rigid Left has increased by 4 percent. The ability of these right-wing media to recruit is unimpressive.

Why have the right-wing media had so little effect? The answer lies in the political orientation of their listeners and the share of media users Fox attracts compared to the many other media outlets. In the first place, as of 2016, only 6 percent of the public listened regularly to Russ Limbaugh. In Table 7.2, we see that the most popular commentator in the history of Fox News, Bill O'Reilly, had a viewership of 17 percent in 2016 (before he retired). (Hannity

TABLE 7.2 Media Watched Regularly 2016

	Total Percent Who Watch	Strong Liberal	Ordinary Liberal	Bi-ideological	Ordinary Conservative	Strong Conservative	No Belief System
Fox News (O'Reilly)	17%	1%	5%	16%	23%	40%	3%
NBC (Lester Holt)	23%	17%	18%	33%	32%	17%	30%
CBS	18%	13%	19%	33%	30%	17%	9%
ABC	19%	11%	18%	36%	26%	13%	24%
CNN (Cooper)	17%	19%	21%	19%	15%	10%	19%
MSNBC (Maddow)	10%	26%	10%	13%	9%	1%	4%
Fallon	20%	28%	25%	13%	9%	21%	18%
Kimmel	13%	19%	18%	13%	11%	5%	10%
Colbert	11%	31%	8%	4%	10%	1%	6%

Percent of ideological bloc who watch.
Source: Answer to ANES question "Which of these television programs do you watch regularly?"

has only 6 percent). The programs with a strong liberal slant—MSNBC's Rachel Maddow and late-evening talk shows (Fallon, Kimmel, and Colbert)—have an audience that averages about 16 percent *each*. Since Fallon, Kimmel, and Colbert are on at the same time and each one is getting an audience of about a 16 percent, all three combined have an audience of about 48 percent. (One may question my inclusion of the late-evening hosts but they do present a great deal of news although it is laced with humor.)

The traditional evening news networks (ABC, CBS, NBC) remain a very large source of news. An average of 15 percent watches at least one of these evening news programs, giving the three of them combined a 45 percent viewership.[4] Note in Table 7.2 that the audience for these traditional programs is very balanced ideologically with about equal number of liberals and conservatives (with slightly more conservatives). They also draw an unusually high percentage of Bi-ideologicals and those with No Belief System, the very people that would be most susceptible to persuasion and recruitment by the Fox channel. Thus, the bi or neutral ideologues expose themselves to media that has no slant.

CNN, which has a following as large as O'Reilly did, is relatively unbiased although it does attract a slight disproportion of liberals. If we add all the "balanced" news outlets (traditional and CNN) together we get about 50 percent. Thus, half the public subscribes to neutral media and half to slanted. The half that watch slanted news are mostly liberals.

We see in Table 7.2 another reason that Fox News has not won more adherents to the conservative cause; more than half of their viewers are already conservatives with an especially high number (40 percent) being Strong Conservatives. Fox News is preaching to the choir. *If Fox News is a major force in the political world, it is only because it is considered so by the political elite.*

Cause of a Paralyzed Congress

In Figure 7.2, we see an electorate that is half Rigid (25 percent in each partisan direction) and that proportion has changed very little in the last twenty-four years. It probably has remained nearly the same since the New Deal in the 1930s. The New Deal government programs went against everything Republicans believe in, namely, limited government (with low taxes), individual responsibility, free market economy, against unions, and against regulation. Republicans have been trying to undo the New Deal ever since the 1930s, but that partisan divide has not caused a total breakdown and an inability to govern. Total paralysis is a recent phenomenon.

Prior to 2008, Congress had always gotten things done. In many cases it took a long time, but they muddled through and dealt with the problems of the time. This was accomplished despite the ideological differences between Republicans and Democrats and the separation of powers government structure that makes law-making very difficult when one or both of the legislative bodies and/or the White House are in the hands of the opposite party—when there is divided government.

Let us look at those times when stalemate is most likely—when there was divided government. Yet on numerous of those occasions, the parties have worked together. Presidents have introduced measures that run counter to their ideological predispositions, or Congress has supported proposals of Presidents who had opposing beliefs. For example, Republicans generally do not support public projects, yet in the 1950s, a massive public works project—the Interstate highway system—was begun by a Republican president, Eisenhower. Government subsidies to the very poor, which was first proposed by the liberal Democrat, George McGovern, was established by Richard Nixon in the form of the Earned Income Tax Credit (EIC). Nixon also established the Environmental Protection Agency (EPA). Reagan succeeded in ending the Cold War by winning the arms race with USSR. This required very large defense expenditures which liberals do not like but nonetheless the appropriations were passed by a Democratic Congress. On many other occasions, Reagan worked with Democratic leader Tip O'Neal. Ronald Reagan also established a commission to study the Social Security system to find ways to make sure Social Security funds would be available in the future. President George H. W. Bush increased taxes. Bill Clinton severely tightened requirements for receiving aid for dependent children with the Welfare to Work law. President George W. Bush provided access to prescription drugs for the elderly and greatly extended the federal government's role in education with No Child Left Behind. When the Great Recession occurred at the end of George W. Bush's term in 2008, both parties worked to pass the Economic Stimulus Act of 2008.

What has happened recently to bring Congress to an almost complete standstill? It is a problem that has been manufactured by leaders inside the Beltway.

The paralysis of Congress began in earnest when Barack Obama was elected president in 2008. On the night he was elected, Republican Party leaders were meeting to plan strategies to block him. As Senate Majority Leader, Mitch McConnell, later put it "My number one priority is making sure president Obama is a one-term president." The main pillars of their strategy were:

1   Threaten to filibuster everything.
2   Not act on confirmation of President Obama's choices to fill key administrative and judicial positions.
3   Impose iron-fisted discipline to ensure Republican legislators voted the party line.
4   Enforce discipline by threatening to end a defector's political career with a *well-financed* primary opponent. This new and powerful method of enforcing disciple was made possible by the *Citizens United* case, which allows unlimited contributions. Thus, "well-financed" is easily arranged.

The Filibuster

Up until 1917, a senator could debate a measure endlessly. This was dramatized by Jimmy Stewart in the well-known movie *Mr. Smith Goes to Washington*. In 1917, the Senate passed the Cloture Rule, which provided for the ending of debate if a supermajority of senators voted to do so. That supermajority is now sixty.

After Obama was elected and the majority of Senators were Democrats, the Minority Leader threatened to filibuster virtually every bill. The Majority Leader, Harry Reid, was very concerned that filibusters would slow the work of the Senate and therefore he did not want to bring up a measure unless it was "filibuster proof." The way to do this was to work on a bill until it had the support of sixty members—enough to stop a filibuster. Most of the time the sixty votes could not be found. A few severely watered-down measures (the Affordable Care Act and the Dodd–Frank bank regulation bill) did finally get sixty supporters.[5]

Thus, the mere *threat* of a filibuster made it necessary to have sixty votes to pass measures. The Republican's constant threat of a filibuster brought the process of lawmaking to a halt. And it was done so often that it became standard practice. From then on—to this day—all Senators, Republican or Democrat alike, simply assume a measure must have sixty-vote support or there is no point introducing it. For all intents and purposes, the Constitution has been amended to read "A three-fifths vote is needed to enact any legislation."[6]

When the Republicans took control of the House as a result of the 2010 election, a new way to block Obama was introduced. This was to pass everything with just Republican votes. Nothing would be considered that was not pure Republicanism. However, a major hitch developed. In the 2010 election, the Tea Party was born. About forty of its candidates were elected to Congress. The Speaker of the House, Boehner, needed their votes if he was going to raise a majority solely from the ranks of Republicans. That meant that this extremely conservative Tea Party group had immense bargaining power. At one point, for instance, Speaker Boehner was caught between bargaining for a budget that would meet the approval of President Obama on one hand and the Tea Party caucus on the other. Little or nothing could get done in this no-win situation.[7] (The Tea Party caucus later became known as the Freedom Caucus.)

This pure, party-line voting strategy boomeranged on the Republicans when Trump was elected. One of Trump's earliest priorities was to repeal and replace the Affordable Care Act. However, the Freedom Caucus insisted on certain provisions in the replacement legislation. These provisions were not acceptable to some of the regular Republican congressmen and senators. The bill failed. The Republicans were unable to fulfill their campaign promise to "Repeal and Replace" Obama Care.

House and Senate leaders enforce the strict party discipline necessary to achieve "pure" Republican legislation by threatening to force members to run in a primary against a well- financed opponent if they step out of line. The opponent in the primary is financed by wealthy donors and conservative PACS. These large donations are made possible by the Supreme Court's decision in the *Citizens United* case.

Another major source of alienation and tension between the parties in Congress was the failure of Republican leaders in the Senate to do their Constitutional duty of giving advice and consent. During the Obama years, the Senate often greatly delayed acting on his nominations for key positions. For example, positions on the National Labor Relations Board and the Civil Rights Commission were not acted on for over a year. When the Democratic Congress passed a bill (Dodd–Frank) that called for a Consumer Protection Agency, Republicans refused to consider someone to head it. The most egregious use of advice and consent delay was to thwart the President's nomination of a justice to fill a vacant position of the Supreme Court. The Republican Senate refused to even talk to President Obama's nominee, Merrick Garland. This left an empty seat on the Supreme Court for over a year. How can there be comity and compromise in that belligerent atmosphere?

Another reason that Congress is so polarized is that many moderate Republicans, such as Maine Senator Olympia Snowe, have retired. They could no longer stand the hostile and uncompromising atmosphere.

The extent of polarization in Congress that is shown in Figure 7.1 is misleading. With the threat of being challenged in a primary that could end their career, many congressmen and senators vote for measures that they personally do not fully agree with. They would have been willing to work with Democrats and compromise. Roll-call votes cannot measure the true ideological *thinking* of congressmen and senators and thus do not reveal the true degree of ideological division in Congress.

Paralysis in Congress could be ended overnight if Congressional leaders would:

1   Restore procedural rules so that Cloture could be invoked only after debate on the floor had begun. If sixty votes for Cloture could not be found right away and a prolonged filibuster ensued, so be it. The longest filibuster in history was fifty-seven days.[8] *Better to have delay and achieve legislation than have a bill killed before it is even considered.*
2   Republican leaders should seek support for measures by looking across the aisle and not by just looking into the ranks of the Freedom Caucus.
3   Whip the vote, but not by threatening political death at the hands of a well-financed primary challenger.
4   Perform the Constitutional duty to give advice and consent without deliberate delay.

Notes

1 Recall that Ordinary Liberals and Ordinary Conservatives do not have polar opposite beliefs so they can be combined into one Malleable group.
2 Eight percent of the Rigid Right did not vote for Trump.
3 Strong Democrats went down from 18 percent in 1992 to 13 percent in 2016. The reason the combined Rigid Left increased 4 percent is because of the large increase in Strong Liberals (see Figure 6.4). The 5 percent increase in the Rigid Right was mainly a result of an increase in Strong Republicans.
4 About one-third of those who are interested in traditional news broadcasting mentioned more than one of the stations. They were not counted more than once.
5 Dodd-Frank was watered down by not clearly preventing "too big to fail," and the ACA did not include effective means to assure insurance companies that almost everyone would buy insurance—something that was necessary to provide a big enough pool of purchasers to spread the risk and allow for affordable rates.
6 At the beginning of the 111th Congress in 2011, a group of Democratic senators proposed new rules that would eliminate the pre-emptive filibuster, but most Democrats, including Harry Reid, opposed that change. Both parties want the power to obstruct if they are in the minority.
7 Mann and Ornstein present an excellent case study of the Freedom Caucus' power to obstruct when Obama and Boehner were trying to arrive at a budget agreement in 2011 in *It's Even Worse That It Looks: How the American Constitutional System Collided with the New Politics of Extremism*.
8 It was the 1964 Civil Rights Act that was filibustered for fifty-seven days. Was the wait worth it?

Reference

Mann, Thomas E., and Norman J. Ornstein. 2012. *It's Even Worse That It Looks: How the American Constitutional System Collided with the New Politics of Extremism*. New York: Basic Books.

CONCLUSIONS

In this book, I have found that if you know (1) what a voter thinks about each candidate, (2) what issues the voter is concerned with and the party thought best to handle the problem, and (3) the party the voter identifies with, you can predict that person's vote choice if you know how much weight the voters, on average, gave to each of these factors when making their decision. I developed a mathematical model that estimates those weights. The vote of 95 percent of respondents can be predicted using this model. This assumes that open-ended questions are used to measure attitudes toward candidates and issues. This type a question allows voters to tell you what they are thinking and it is this thinking that results in a voting decision.

I found that knowing the demographic characteristics of the voters or the reactions they have to words presented to them in polls cannot explain their vote.

Change from one election to the next is a result of short-term forces—the candidates and the issues. Each election presents the voter with new factors—new candidates[1] and new issues. Each election is unique. Chapter 5 showed that the importance of each factor (each component) in each election. Sometimes it is a candidate who is most important, sometimes it is issues, and sometimes it is party identification. My model has worked nearly perfectly for six decades and there is no reason to believe it will not continue to work for decades into the future. The net total of the components, calculated using my method, came within ±1 percent of the actual vote.

Finally, we saw that the result of the previous election is a very temporary moving point that cannot be a base from which to measure change in the current election.

The Role of Ideology

Political scientists, political analysts, and party leaders see the electorate as arrayed along a bell-shaped left–right spectrum. Survey questions, such as "are you a strong liberal, moderate liberal, middle of the road, moderate conservative or strong conservative," were designed to measure this spectrum. The distribution of responses to these survey questions confirmed the bell-shaped distribution. In Chapter 6, I showed that responses to these ideological identity questions were highly unreliable—that over half of the voters did not know what a liberal or a conservative was and were responding randomly. Those who did not know what these academic terms meant often avoided appearing uniformed by saying they were middle-of-the road (thus the bulge in the middle of the bell-shaped curve). These middle-of-the-road responses are meaningless—most of these respondents could not be middle-of-the-road since they are not aware that there is a road (a liberal–conservative spectrum).

Also, I found a way to separate those who were guessing from the real ideologues and saw that real ideological identity is not distributed along a bell-shaped liberal–conservative continuum (see Figure 8.1).

The important thing to know about the ideology of the electorate is not so much their identity as the substantive beliefs that they hold. I found a

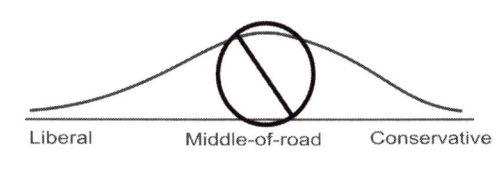

FIGURE 8.1   Liberal–conservative Spectrum.

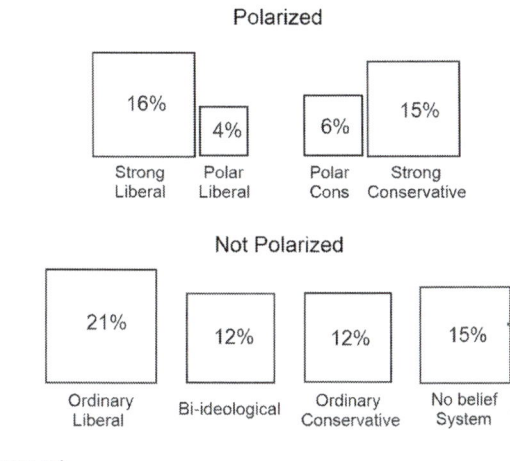

FIGURE 8.2   2016 Blocs.

way to measure these belief systems that is highly reliable and was tested for validity in a number of ways (see Chapter 6). The electorate is divided into seven blocs of beliefs and one bloc with No Belief System. In 2016, the ideological composition of the American electorate looked like what is shown in Figure 8.2.

The Polarized blocs have diametrically opposite beliefs, the Not Polarized blocs have different, but not opposing, beliefs.

The Rigid and the Malleable Voters

I found that about half of the electorate is Rigid—unmovable. Half of these Rigid are Rigid Right consisting of Strong Conservatives and/or Strong Republicans. Half are Rigid Left consisting of Strong Liberals and/or Strong Democrats. Thus, Republican candidates can count on a quarter of the electorate—the Rigid Right—to vote for them in every election. Democratic candidates can count on the quarter of the electorate who are Rigid Left. That leaves half the electorate who are open to persuasion—the Malleable. These are the Weak Democrats, Weak Republicans, Independents, Ordinary Liberals, Ordinary Conservatives, the Bi-ideologicals, and those with No Belief System.

We saw in Chapter 4 that the ideology of the candidate was seldom mentioned in the profiles.[2] But we found in Chapter 3 and in Table 6.2 that it is used by the strongest ideologues (the Rigid) when evaluating candidates and choosing their issue concerns. These Rigid voters have incorporated their ideology into these evaluations. They use explicit reasons, not general categories like "liberal" or "conservative" to articulate these evaluations.

Ideology and party are not major influences on the Malleable and it is they who determine the outcome of the election. Almost none of the Malleable voters measure candidates by how liberal or conservative they are. They are interested in the character, experience, and leadership ability, etc. of the candidates plus how the candidate will deal with problems. Yet most political analysts use ideology as a major rubric to explain elections.

Summary of Major Findings

Coalitions

Most political analysts talk of coalitions of demographic groups, but we have seen that demographics do not explain vote. It is the Issue Publics that are the important groups to appeal to; candidates need to *build coalitions of Issue Publics* and that means taking clear positions on issues. Even a small Issue Public of 3 percent could spell the difference between winning and losing in close elections. Therefore, candidates need to take positions on many issues.

The Motivation for Issue Concerns

In Chapter 3 we learned that the issues voters are concerned with were seldom based on self-interest. For example, in the 1960s, knowing someone was white told you nothing about their attitude toward civil rights, knowing someone had a home did not mean they were not concerned about the homeless, knowing that someone could afford health care insurance did not mean that they were any the less concerned about the general problem of health insurance, knowing that someone did not have children of school age did not mean they are not concerned with education. The environment and drugs were concerns throughout society. Many issues were concerns about the good of the country—defending the country, the national debt, fuel shortages in the 1970s, our prisoners in Iran in 1980, concern about divisiveness in 2016. Many concerns were based on beliefs and values. For example, half the country are liberals who believe in helping others and in equality—thus they support minority rights even though they are not in a minority group, and they are concerned about poverty even if they themselves are not poor. (All of the issues mentioned above were the ones most often cited as important problems during the years of this study.)

Polarization

Only half the electorate is polarized (Rigid) yet Congress is almost totally polarized. How is it that a half-polarized electorate is represented by a totally polarized Congress? The answer can be found in Chapter 7.

Some Other Findings

- There is a "steady state" of the electorate between elections when the short-term forces that come to the fore at election time are not at play. If a vote were taken in this "steady state," it would be based on party identification alone. Knowing what the vote would be in this "steady state" provides a good baseline from which to measure the amount and direction of short-term forces in the current election.
- Democratic Party identifiers have steadily decreased since 1992 yet strong liberals have increased from 6 percent in 1992 to 16 percent in 2016. The reasons for this inverse relationship are explained in Chapters 1 and 2. Basically, new generations of liberals have not been attracted to the Democratic Party since the party no longer flies the liberal banner and the party has, for decades, directed its messages to the middle class and ignored the 30 percent who identify with the working class and the 30 percent who do not identify with any class.
- When looking at why a candidate won, it is important to remember that it may have less to do with the candidate's popularity than the dislike of

the opponent. Goldwater, Carter (in 1980), and H. Clinton were widely disliked, which greatly helped the winner.

- Gun control (the Brady Bill and a ban on assault rifles) became law[3] under Clinton and he received almost no unfavorable comments about these laws in the 1996 election.
- Abortion and taxes are not important issues as far as the public is concerned. There was no mention of either of them in the list of Issue Publics in Chapter 3. Major tax cuts by Reagan were not mentioned when voters evaluated him and the tax cuts by George W. Bush drew only scant praise. We also saw that Mondale's call for a tax increase was only a minor reason why he lost.
- Right-wing media, such as Fox News and Rush Limbaugh, have been on the air since the 1990s, yet the proportion of conservatives and Republicans in the electorate has only increased slightly; there is no sign of recruitment. On the other hand, the proportion of strong liberals has greatly increased.

Following Are Examples of Voters' Attitudes Toward Candidates Revealed by Asking Open-ended Questions

1   John F. Kennedy almost lost because he was a Catholic. He managed to win because he started with an advantage—48 percent of the electorate were Democratic Party identifiers at that time.
2   Gerald Ford had a boost in support from those who felt he had done the right thing in pardoning Nixon. He almost won.
3   McGovern and Dukakis did not lose because they were liberals.
4   Mondale did not lose because he suggested increasing taxes.
5   Reagan's conservative policies were disliked by as many as liked them. He had no net favorability. He won big in 1984 because he saw a "shining city on the hill"—he gave people hope.
6   George H. W. Bush's promise of "No New Taxes" did not resonate. No one paid any attention to it.
7   The data show that Trump is an aberration in many ways. The 2016 election was the first time that voters put almost all weight on the candidates when making their decisions. Way over half of the electorate was appalled by Trump (and that was before he took office). One respondent to the ANES survey said, insightfully:

> The climate in this country is how divided we are. I think there is a lot more racists and bigots than I thought there were. I think Trump brought this out and made people feel comfortable in voicing their racist views and misogynist views as well.[4]

When asked what the most important problems were in 2016, almost all the problems stemmed from Trump. Divisiveness and hatred between groups was a leading concern. Racism was the next most leading concern.

And Trump himself was often mentioned as a problem. Trump did not win the White House with majority support—he had only 46 percent of the vote. His election was due to two flukes: being lucky enough to have an opponent who was disliked and the vagaries of the Electoral College.

Using Open-ended Questions

If candidates and pollsters would like to know *accurately and substantively* what is on voters' minds during a campaign, they would have to use open-ended questions. However, administering open-ended questions is difficult and expensive. Open-ended questions require skilled interviewers and the answers obtained must be coded into summarizing expressions that reflect the actual verbatim answer. (The profiles in Chapter 4 are examples of coded verbatims.) All this is time-consuming and expensive. That is why open-ended surveys are seldom used.[5] But they could be used if the clients for this information were more patient. Instead of investing in unreliable polls every week or so, pollsters could save the money they would have spent on them and spend it on less frequent surveys using open-ended questions. The information gained from these less-frequent polls would be far more valuable. Any pollster using those questions would gain the reputation that comes with accuracy and substantive information about voters' thoughts.

Any campaign manager that uses open-ended questions in surveys will have a much better chance of winning. They will know what Issue Publics to appeal to and how to improve their candidate's image.

The Mandate

Democracy is supposed to be based on the will of the people and elections are the way that will is expressed. Elections are supposed to give government a mandate. But after every election there have always been several different interpretations of the mandate by various political analysts. The methods of analysis in this book provide a way to know what the voters had in mind and how important each component was. From now on, *we can know with certainty what the mandate is.*

But under current rules in the Senate, that mandate will never be acted on. Almost all proposed legislation needs the approval of at least sixty senators before debate can begin. A minority of forty-one can block everything. For all intents and purposes, the Constitution has been amended to read "Passage of legislation shall require a three-fifth vote of the Senate." What if that clause had been in the original Constitution? How many laws in our history would not have been passed because they needed sixty votes?

It matters not which party has a majority; unless it has a majority of sixty or more almost nothing will move in the Senate. "Regular order" needs to become "proper order" in which *debate comes before stopping debate.* Those who want to filibuster should be able to take the floor and debate at length if they have a particularly strong concern and are willing to make the effort. This upholds minority rights. It may take days, even weeks, before enough votes for cloture are obtained and debate stopped. At that point, a simple majority vote is all that would be needed to pass the legislation. *Better to have a procedure that allows measures with majority (51 percent) support to pass, albeit sometimes slowly because of a filibuster, rather than have all measures dead on arrival because they need 60 votes.*

But unless the leaders of both parties in Congress agree to change the rules to do away with pre-emptive cloture, the majority that wins the election will not rule. The people will have spoken, but Congressional leaders will not hear.

Notes

1 Incumbent presidents who run for re-election are new in that they are now much better known and are now judged on a major new quality—their performance in office.
2 It is interesting to note that Philip Converse, in his study of levels of conceptualization presented in Chapter 10 of *The American Voter*, found few voters used the terms "liberal" or "conservative" when evaluating candidates. Subsequent researchers using the Converse method also found little articulation of the terms "liberal" or "conservative."
3 These laws were sunset ten years later.
4 Since Trump's election, there has been much written and said about the "tribalism" and the division of American society. This is not the America I found in the ANES interviews. The behavior of a few that has been encouraged and legitimized by Trump will go underground again when he no longer is in office.
5 Ronald Reagan's pollster, Dick Wirthlin, often use open-ended questions. Gallup periodically uses a most important problem question in an abbreviated form.

APPENDIX A

MY MODEL EQUATION AND THE COMPONENTS

The Model Equation in the Introduction is based Donald Stokes' analysis, which was first presented in Stokes (1958) and later in Chapters 3 and 4 of *The American Voter* (Campbell et al., 1960). The only major difference between his use of multiple regression and mine is that Stokes used six independent variables and I only used four. Mine are attitude toward the Democratic candidate, attitude toward the Republican candidate, most important problem (MIP), and party identification (PID). I will discuss his six components later.

Attitudes toward Candidates

To obtain a numerical measure of attitude toward candidate, each positive comment about the candidate was scored +1, each negative comment, −1. Up to five positive and five negative comments about each candidate were recorded by the interviewer. The measure of attitude toward candidate was the net (algebraic) sum of these comments. For example, if a respondent said two good things about a candidate and one bad, his/her net score was +1; if a respondent said two good things about a candidate and two bad things, the net score was 0. If a respondent said three good things and no bad things, the score would have been +3, etc.

Early on, the Stokes method was criticized because regression analysis assumes interval data (equal intervals between each score) and this is not true of each comment made in response to the open-ended candidate question. The first comment or two may be far more important than further comments. To mitigate the problem of assuming that each comment is of equal importance, that is, worth one point on an interval scale, I truncated the *net* scores so that they ranged from +2 to −2 instead of +5 to −5. The difference between the scores on the resulting five-point scale (+2, +1, 0, −1, −2) can be considered interval.

This truncation also meant that the more verbose respondents were put on an equal footing with the less forthcoming. Furthermore, this truncation reduced the amount of unexplained error. Without truncation, scores beyond 2 were probably not as important as the first two in contributing to the explained variation (R^2). These addition scores created unexplained variation in the system.[1]

PID and MIP

Note that we are working with bipolar dimensions. Mathematically, it is necessary to have a way to distinguish partisan direction and that is done with +'s and −'s. When Stokes performed his regression analysis in the 1950s, the Democrats were the ascendant party so he set up his equation so that a plus would represent the Democratic direction and minus the Republican direction. I simply followed that precedent.

PID was measured on a five-point scale as follows:[2]

+2 Strong Democrat
+1 Weak Democrat
 0 Independent
−1 Weak Republican
−2 Strong Republican

When coding the MIP, the issue was given a partisan valence by coding it +1 if the respondent thought the Democratic Party would be best able to handle a problem; if the party best able was thought to be the Republican, the code was −1. If neither party was thought able to deal the problem, the code was "0."

The Dependent Variable

I coded a Democratic vote with +.5 and a Republican vote with −.5. When the Model Equation produces an estimate of vote, the result is going to be somewhere along the following scale—a scale running from +1.0 (full support for the Democrat to 0.1 (extremely little support for the Democratic candidate) and from −0.1 (little support) to −1.0 (full support for the Republican candidate). A zero would indicate a Toss-up (see Figure A.1).

The midpoint on the positive side of the hypothetical scale would be +.5, and on the negative side, −.5. These are the best estimates we have available to use in solving the Model Equation.

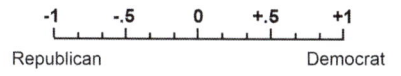

FIGURE A.1 Vote Scale.

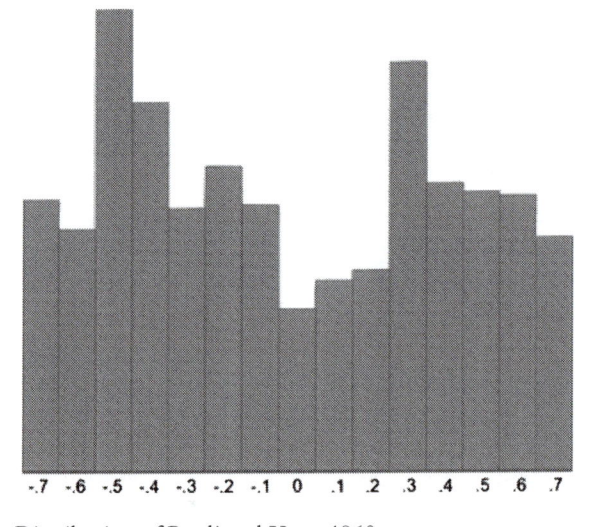

FIGURE A.2 Distribution of Predicted Vote, 1960.

Many political scientists believe that multiple regression cannot be used if the dependent variable is a dichotomy. The reasons for this concern are (1) that the values of the dependent variable will not be continuous and (2) the predicted values of some individuals will be outside of the range of +1 or −1.

I tested to see if these problems occurred in my analyses. Using 1960 data as an example, we see that the results were continuous and no case was outside the range of +1 or −1 (Figure A.2).

The Components

Stokes found a way to measure the amount each component of the vote contributed to moving the electorate in the Democratic direction or in the Republican direction. To find the value of each component, Stokes multiplied the mean of each component by its weight (regression coefficient). The result was the amount the whole electorate was moved in one partisan direction or the other by that attitude or component. When the net amount of the six components in Stokes' equation were added, the result was the amount the whole electorate was moved away from a 50–50 position. This is explained in detail with geometric figures in his 1958 article.

The six components that Stokes used were: Attitude toward the Democratic candidate (Stevenson), the Republican candidate (Eisenhower), Group-related Attitude, Attitude on Domestic Issues, Attitude on Foreign Issues, and Attitude toward Parties as Managers of Government. However, this set of categories was flawed.

At the time Stokes did his analysis of the 1952 and 1956 elections, the MIP question was not in the ANES surveys and so he had no question that specifically asked about issues. His data about issues was based on the open-ended questions about likes and dislikes of the candidates and a question that asked for likes and dislikes of the parties. This meant that his domestic and foreign issue components were not based on an explicit question about problems or issues, but were the incidental by-products of questions about candidates and parties.

Furthermore, I have learned that many of the issues that are forthcoming when respondents are asked about candidates are issues that are an integral part of candidates' images and *would not be issues if that candidate had not run*. The clearest examples of this were the fear of World War III when Goldwater ran in 1964 (rattling the nuclear saber), and Trump introducing the issues of hate, racism, and divisiveness in 2016. Other examples are Ford's pardon of Nixon, the hostage crisis 1980 (which was blamed on Carter), in 1984 Reagan's methods of dealing with USSR, in 1988 the national debt (which was run up by Reagan). Also, in 1988, the war in Nicaragua (contras) was an issue since Vice President Bush was thought to have been involved with it. The Willie Horton furlough would not have been an issue in 1988 if Dukakis had not vetoed a measure that would have prevented murderers from having furloughs. Benghazi would not have been an issue if Hillary Clinton had not been Secretary of State. All of these issues were part of the candidate's image and were not stand-alone issues.

Also, Stokes' Group-related component is part of the candidate image. One of the many reasons voters liked a Democratic candidate was because he or she supported the common man or the working man. Some Republican candidates were disliked for being too favorable to the rich. But this group-related criterion was not applied universally to all candidate—it was not a constant component. It is part of only some candidate images and is candidate-oriented.

Finally, it does not matter whether an issue is domestic or foreign, it has the same effect on voting decisions depending on its valence.

Also, Stokes' Parties as Managers of Government component was a component unique to the 1952 election when Harry Truman was the incumbent president. He had been accused of too much cronyism. A corruption issue never arose again with any other candidate and should not have been made into a separate category in the first place.

In sum, anything that is said in response to the like and dislike of the candidates' question is part of the voter's image of the candidate and should not be taken away from the candidate and moved into a separate category.

Measuring the Impact of Party Identification

I have read through thousands of ANES interviews and noticed from the verbatim responses that when respondents are asked for their likes and dislikes of parties, the question they hear is: why are you a Democrat/

Republican?[3] Respondents often mention issues that parties have histori-
cally promoted. Stokes separated these issue-oriented comments *made about
parties* and put them with *current* domestic and foreign issues. It is best to
measure party identification explicitly and see how much it influences the
vote, as I have done.

Most importantly, issues obtained with the open-ended MIP question are
issues that stem mostly from events and conditions, and are independent of the
candidates and the parties. They are "stand alone" and exist in voters' minds
based on their concerns. They need to be measured separately.

Spuriousness

Spuriousness occurs when a third variable is highly correlated with both the
independent variable and the dependent variable and thus causes covariation
between the independent and dependent variables. All apparent correlations
between an independent and dependent variable should be tested for spuriousness by controlling for possible third variables. This control will cause the
apparent correlation to become very small or even disappear if the relation is
spurious. One of the beauties of multiple regression is that the effect of each independent variable is measured while the other independent variables are being
controlled or held constant.

We saw in the Introduction that the relation between ideology and vote was
not significant when ideology was introduced as an independent variable into
the Model Equation. Using the 1988 ANES data, let us look at what happens
to the bivariate correlation between ideology and vote (.40) when a third variable, which is highly correlated with both ideology and vote, is held constant
or controlled (Figure A.3).

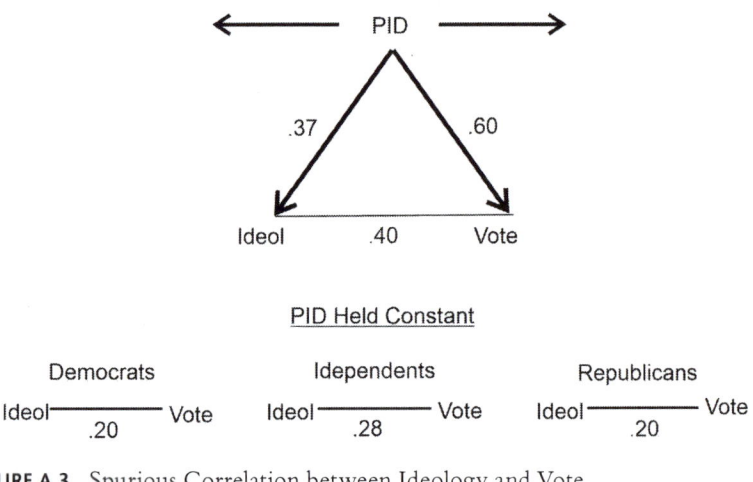

FIGURE A.3 Spurious Correlation between Ideology and Vote.

Figure A.3 is a triangle in which each side represents the correlation (tau-b) between each of the three variables being examined. Note that there is a strong relation between party identification (PID) and ideology (IDEOL) and between PID and VOTE. These relations are shown by large arrows in Figure A.3. There are horizontal arrows on each side of PID, which indicate that party identification varies back and forth between those who are Democrats, Republicans, and Independents. Since PID is strongly linked to both IDEOL and VOTE, this variation in PID is transmitted to IDEOL and VOTE and they vary as well (.40 correlation). When we hold PID constant (as shown below the triangle figure), the relation between IDEOL and VOTE is significantly reduced to about .20. The .40 *bivariate* relation between IDEOL and VOTE was spurious— caused by a third variable, PID.

Conclusion

In evaluating my Model Equation and my component analysis, the reader may find fault with some of the mathematical details and methodological assumptions, but note that these methods were carefully validated and predicted vote almost perfectly. The Model Equation predicted the vote of 95 percent of the respondents. The components analysis found the net movement of the electorate away from 50–50 and that result was within ±1 percent of the actual vote.

Notes

1 This was born out of experimenting with the two-point scales, three-point scales, four-point scales, and five-point scales. The R^2 was greater the more the truncation.
2 Note that we are working with bipolar dimensions. Mathematically, it is necessary to have a way to distinguish partisan direction and that is done with +'s and −'s. When Stokes performed his regression analysis in the 1950s, the Democrats were the ascendant party so he set up his equation so that a plus would represent the Democratic direction and minus the Republican direction. I simply followed that precedent.
3 The authors of *The American Voter* concluded that Independents "have somewhat poorer knowledge of the issues, their image of the candidates is fainter." Naturally, Independents would have less to say if they are, in essence, asked "why are you a Democrat/Republican?"

References

Campbell, Angus, Philip E. Converse, Warren E. Miller, and Donald E. Stokes. 1960. *The American Voter*. New York: Wiley.
Stokes, Donald E. 1958. "Components of the Electoral Decision." *The American Political Science Review*, 62 (2): 367–387.

APPENDIX B

CALCULATING THE AMOUNT OF RANDOM RESPONSE

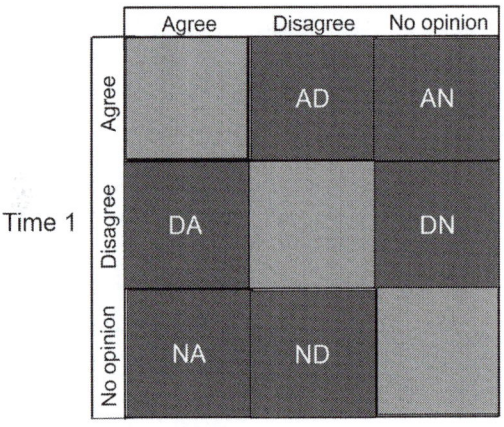

FIGURE B.1 Time 1–Time 2 Figure.

Almost all in the black cells were responding randomly—real attitudes should not change from Time 1 to Time 2 and those in the black cells have changed. The gray (no-change) cells represent two types of respondents—those who have real attitudes and those who were responding randomly but happened to end up in no-change cells by chance. The probability of landing in any cell in a 3×3 Time 1–Time 2 contingency table (as shown above) is 1/9. Each issue has a certain number of random responders—a certain propensity for random response—depending on how many respondents have a real attitude regarding the issue and how many do not. This propensity for random response to a particular issue question can be estimated by observing the proportion of cases in the six black cells—almost all of whom have responded.[1] We can observe 6/9th of the random responders and thus determine the propensity to respond randomly on this issue. From this information, we can calculate the total number of random responders. That total divided by the number of cases gives the proportion of random responders.

We can use the following formula to calculate the total number of random responders.

By definition: $OT = \frac{6}{9} TET = \frac{2}{3} TET$ Therefore: $TET = \frac{3}{2} OT$

Percent TET = TET/N × 100

where:

OT = Observed Turnover—the number of respondents who were observed in the turnover cells (the black cells).

TET = Total Estimated turnover or random response.

N = Number of cases in table.

The Black and White Method

In his well-known article on belief systems, "The Nature of Belief Systems in Mass Publics," Philip Converse found a way to find the number of random responders to fixed-choice questions. It was called the "black and white" method but it required a three-wave panel, which is very rare and was based on regression analysis. My method requires only two-wave panels and is based on probability.

Note

1 In doing the test—retests and observing the number of cases in each black cell, I found that the number of cases in each of these cells was roughly the same—within one and a half standard deviations of the number expected (6/9th). This demonstrates that the propensity for random response is consistent throughout the table. Occasionally, one cell would have an unusual number of cases in it, but the cell that contained this aberration varied randomly.

APPENDIX C

MY METHOD OF MEASURING BELIEF SYSTEMS

There are two aspects to ideology, identity, and belief systems. The measure of identity was discussed in Chapter 6. This Appendix will explain my method of measuring belief systems.

Philip Converse was the "father" of the study of belief systems. His seminal work *The Nature of Belief Systems in Mass Publics* (Converse, 1964) greatly influenced all studies of belief systems ever since. Converse did the following:

1   He defined a belief system as "a configuration of ideas and attitudes in which the elements are bound together by some form of constraint or functional interdependence." Converse goes on to say that "constraint, for example, is that if a person is opposed to expansion of social security, he is probably a conservative and is probably opposed as well to any nationalization of private industries, federal aid to education, progressive income taxes and so forth." Note that the idea elements that Converse expects to be "constrained" are based on his beliefs about "what goes with what" (as he said on p. 239). Thus, he assumed that ordinary citizens form a belief system by interconnecting issues using the same logic, awareness, and conceptual knowledge as he had. But ordinary citizens may structure their beliefs in ways that differ from those of the political elite.

2   Converse used contemporary issues as measures of elements of belief systems. But *beliefs* are *long-term* attitudes that are central in an attitude structure and resist change. Issues come and go. For example, "should electric power be provided by the government or private companies?" was an issue that Converse used in his "Mass Publics" article at a time when Tennessee Valley Authority (TVA) was being debated. The issue of public power has long since disappeared. Foreign aid was an issue in 1950s but has not been

mentioned in recent years, and school integration was a hot topic in the 1960s but has faded since. And so forth.

3   Furthermore, *beliefs* are *general,* neutral (non-polemic), statements that have no specific referent such as a law or specific policy proposal. Contemporary issues are specific policy proposals or laws that address a current issue. For example, the Affordable Care Act is a poor indicator of general belief in government vs. private health insurance since it refers to a specific law—a law that invokes partisanship and attitude toward Obama, not general belief. Another example of why an opinion on a current issue would not be a good measure of a belief is Afghanistan. One would expect conservatives to support taking military action anywhere to defend America. Yet after eight years in Afghanistan, even conservatives were against it.

4   We should also measure values since they are part of belief systems. *Values* are important life goals or societal conditions desired by a person. Values are broad, abstract concepts like freedom, justice, patriotism, family, piety, morality, altruism, and service to others.

In sum, my method of finding belief systems is very different than Converse's:

1   I wanted to find what idea elements ordinary citizens put together to form their own belief systems. I let them decide "what goes with what." I do *not* require ordinary citizens to have the belief systems of the political elite. I define *belief system simply a set of beliefs that voters have brought together on their own.*

2   I used measures of beliefs and values, not contemporary issues, to find the elements of belief systems.

Finding Beliefs and Values

Using the definitions of beliefs and values as criteria,[1] I searched through the ANES surveys from 1992 through 2016 and assembled *all* questions that measured beliefs or values. Only the 1992, 2004, 2012, and 2016 surveys contained enough comparable questions to be used.[2] There were over forty belief and value questions in each of the four studies. With four studies available, it was possible to replicate my method of analysis four times.

Having selected the belief and value questions, the next step was to search for patterns in the data that revealed belief systems. If certain questions were all consistently answered in one ideological direction, that was evidence of a belief system. There was no way to tell ahead of time which questions would be responded to in this systematic manner.

Principal component factor analysis is the best tool to perform this kind of search. I applied this analysis to the belief and value questions to find which items had been answered in the same ideological direction by a substantial number of respondents. This systematic response pattern was revealed by loadings on a factor or underlying dimension. This analysis was performed separately in each of the four studies.

The questions I assembled are shown in Table C.1 with the average[3] principal component loading over the four years.

TABLE C.1 List of All Belief and Value Questions in ANES 1992, 2004, 2012, 2016 Studies with Average Principal Component Loadings

Loading of Principal Component

.48	Defense spending: much less OR greatly increased.
.42	How important is it for the U.S. to have a strong military force in order to be effective in dealing with our enemies?
.01	We would be better off if we just stayed home and did not concern ourselves with the problems in other parts of the world.
.45	How much government regulation of business is good for society? A great deal, a lot, a moderate amount, a little, or none at all.
.30	Do you think the government is getting too powerful, or not getting too strong?
.58	Government should provide fewer services such as health and education OR should it provide more services.
.51	Government should see that every person has a job OR should they get ahead on their own.
.54	Government should make every effort to improve the social and economic position of blacks and other minorities OR government should not make special effort to help minorities because they should help themselves.
.28	Women should have an equal role with men in work force OR woman's place is in the home.
.37	Do you favor or oppose the death penalty for persons convicted of murder?
.40	Government should make it more difficult to buy a gun, less difficult, OR keep rules the same.
.35	Is religion an important part of your life OR not?
.38	The Bible is the actual word of God and is to be taken literally, word for word.
.41	Do you think gay or lesbian couples should be legally permitted to adopt children?
.50	Should same-sex couples be allowed to marry?
.50	We need a strong government to handle today's complex economic problems, OR the free market can handle these problems.
.53	Government has become bigger over the years because it has gotten involved in things that people should do for themselves, OR because the problems we face have become bigger.
.53	The less government, the better OR, there are more things that government should be doing.
.40	When you see the American flag flying does it make you feel extremely good, very good OR not very good.

(Continued)

.30 How strong is your love for your country? extremely strong, very strong, somewhat strong or not very strong.

.20 Have increases in the government's wiretapping powers since September 11, 2001, gone too far, are they just about right, or do they not go far enough?

.53 Please say to what extent you agree or disagree with the following statement: "The government should take measures to reduce differences in income levels."

Social Change

.31 Is being an American extremely important, very important, OR somewhat important?

.38 The newer lifestyles are contributing to the breakdown in our society.

.35 The world is always changing and we should adjust our view of moral behavior to those changes.

.38 The country would have many fewer problems if there were more emphasis on traditional family ties.

Egalitarianism

.39 We should be more tolerant of people who choose to live according to their own moral standards.

.29 Our society should do what is necessary to make sure that everyone has an equal opportunity to succeed.

.52 One of the big problems is that we don't give everyone and equal chance.

.48 The country would be better off if we worried less about how equal people are.

.35 It is not really that big a problem if some people have more of a chance in life than others.

.36 If people were treated more equally we would have many fewer problems.

Altruism

For which of the following programs would you like to see spending increased OR for which would you like to see spending decreased?

.54 Welfare

.30 Social Security

.55 Childcare

.50 Public schools

.53 Aid to the poor

.09 Foreign aid

.57 Improving and protecting the environment

Note: The ANES had a question on abortion in all of the studies, but its loading varied greatly from year to year. I decided to study it separately. The results of that study were presented in Chapter 6.

From this list, I took all questions that loaded at .50 or higher[4] (which are shown in bold). These items are the ones shown in Chapter 6, List 1. As one looks over these items, it is clear that they are all traditional liberal beliefs.[5] The first principal component analysis has revealed the beliefs that make up a liberal belief system.[6]

A Second Dimension

After years of working with factor analysis, I discovered that the first principal component tends to suppress a possible second major factor. If there is a dominate first principal component, it will "overpower" or mask items that may measure a second factor. By removing the items that loaded highly on the first factor and running the analysis again on the remaining items, the items that form the second factor are free to do so, uninfluenced by the first factor items. This method worked extremely well for finding a second principal component. This method is unconventional but it worked beautifully. Throughout the book, blocs of ideologues built from the items that formed the second principle component performed as well as those built on the first component.

Table C.2 contains a list of the items from the original complete set of beliefs (Table C.1) with the items that loaded highly on the first principal component removed. A second principal component analysis was performed on this list and the average loading from that analysis is shown in Table C.2 along with the original loading from Table C.1.

TABLE C.2 Second Principal Component

Original Loading from Table C1	Loading on Second Principal Component	
.48	**.55**	Defense spending: much less OR greatly increased.
.42	**.58**	How important is it for the U.S. to have a strong military force in order to be effective in dealing with our enemies?
.01	.01	We would be better off if we just stayed home and did not concern ourselves with the problems in other parts of the world.
.45	.20	How much government regulation of business is good for society? A great deal, a lot, a moderate amount, a little, or none at all.
.30	.12	Do you think the government is getting too powerful, or not getting too strong?
.28	.37	Women should have an equal role with men in work force OR woman's place is in the home.
.37	.35	Do you favor or oppose the death penalty for persons convicted of murder?
.40	.33	Government should make it more difficult to buy a gun, less difficult, OR keep rules the same.
.35	**.50**	Is religion an important part of your life OR not?

(Continued)

Original Loading from Table C1	Loading on Second Principal Component	
.38	.57	The Bible is the actual word of God and is to be taken literally, word for word.
.41	.60	Do you think gay or lesbian couples should be legally permitted to adopt children?
.50	**.65**	Should same-sex couples be allowed to marry?
.40	**.52**	When you see the American flag flying does it make you feel extremely good, very good OR not very good.
.30	**.50**	How strong is your love for your country? Extremely strong, very strong, somewhat strong or not very strong.
.31	**.50**	Is being an American extremely important, very important, OR somewhat important?
.38	**.56**	The newer lifestyles are contributing to the breakdown in our society.
.35	.33	The world is always changing and we should adjust our view of moral behavior to those changes.
.38	**.56**	The country would have many fewer problems if there were more emphasis on traditional family ties.
.39	.45	We should be more tolerant of people who choose to live according to their own moral standards
.20	.17	Have increases in the government's wiretapping powers since September 11, 2001, gone too far, are they just about right, or do they not go far enough?

For which of the following programs would you like to see spending increased OR for which would you like to see spending decreased?

| .09 | .11 | Foreign aid |
| .02 | .10 | Dealing with crime |

Note that many items that had low loadings in the original factor analysis (using the entire list), now loaded very highly. They were now free of the suppressing effect of the high loading items in the first principal component or factor. For example, "Is religion an important part of your life?" went from .35 on the first to .50 on the second; "How strong is your love of your country?" went from .30 to .50; and "The country would have many fewer problems if there were more emphasis on traditional family ties" went from .38 to .56.

I then took the items that loaded .50 or better on this second component and presented them in List 2 in Chapter 6. As one looks over these items, it is clear that they are all traditional conservative beliefs. The second principle component had revealed the beliefs that made up the conservative belief system of ordinary citizens.

Beliefs That the Public Does Not Think Are Part of a Conservative Belief System

Most political scientists and others in the political elite think the death penalty, less government regulation, no gun control, no foreign aid, and taking measures to fight crime are sure markers of conservatism. The conservatives in the public do not think that way. Note the low loadings for these items on the conservative component analysis.

There were some beliefs that were ideological orphans, that is, loaded on neither liberal nor conservative dimensions. They were questions about an equal role for women, isolationism, and wiretapping.

Conclusions

In evaluating my method of finding ideologues, the reader may find fault with some of the methods, but these methods worked beautifully. The blocs of belief systems that were discovered were validated by comparing them with ideological identity and only a handful of cases were a mismatch (see Table 6.1). And the voting behavior of the Strong Liberals and Strong Conservatives that I discovered was perfectly predictable; close to 100 percent of them voted for the ideologically appropriate candidate (see Table 6.3).

Notes

1 To repeat: *beliefs* are *long-term* attitudes that are central in an attitude structure and resist change. *Beliefs* are *general,* neutral (non-polemic), statements that have no specific referent such as a law or specific policy proposal. *Values* are important life goals or societal conditions desired by a person.

2 The 1996, 2000, and 2008 studies could not be used. The 1996 study was largely made up of a panel that had been interviewed in 1992; it would be redundant to analyze the same respondents twice. The 2000 ANES could not be used since it was administered mainly by phone and therefore question format was different from other ANES studies. The 2008 ANES lacked two important belief questions.

3 Most questions had nearly the same loading in each of the four years, thus averaging was appropriate.

4 A loading of .50 or higher would seem to be an unnecessarily high requirement. Actually, it is a minimum requirement when one considers that loadings are equivalent to Pearson's r and r^2 (.5^2) explains only 25 percent of the variance.

5 In an article I wrote in 2008, I defined liberal and conservative beliefs based on common usage, the writings of liberals and conservatives, and books on ideology. With this knowledge, I was able to identify items on the lists that measured liberal beliefs and which measured conservative beliefs. See (RePass, 2008).

6 There was another question that did load highly on the first dimension, but it was asked in only one study (2012) so it could not be used if the dimension was to be comparable in all four years. That question was "The government should take measures to reduce differences in income levels."

Reference

RePass, David E. 2008. "Searching for Voters on the Liberal-Conservative Continuum, the Infrequent Ideologue and the Missing Middle." *The Forum* 6(2). Berkeley Electronic Press. doi:10.2202/1540-8884.1220

APPENDIX D

DEMOGRAPHIC UNIQUENESS OF THE IDEOLOGICAL BLOCS

Table D.1 shows the demographic characteristics that are significantly over-represented or underrepresented in the various blocs. If a bloc contains a demographic characteristic that is at least 10 percentage points more or 10 percentage points less than the national average, that characteristic is listed, along with the exact percentage by which it differs from the national average. For example, "Male +11" is listed under Strong Liberal, meaning that this ideological bloc contains 11 percent more males than the national percentage of males.

We see that Strong Liberals tend to be young (39 or less and not over 65), very highly educated, and non-religious. Strong Conservatives tend not to be young, are well educated, and quite wealthy (high income and own stock). Those 39 years old or less are overrepresented among Ordinary Liberals along with an unusual number of low-income people. Ordinary Liberals tend not to own stock. Ordinary Conservatives tend to be older religious fundamentalists who go to church every week. The Bi-ideologicals have the same religious orientation as Ordinary Conservatives, but are quite different from any of the other ideological blocs in that they have much less education and have little wealth. Whites are overrepresented among Strong Liberals as well as Strong Conservatives, while blacks and Hispanics are overrepresented among Ordinary Liberals and Bi-ideologicals.

The South is often characterized as being conservative politically and fundamentalist in religion. It may come as somewhat of a surprise to find that Strong and Ordinary Conservatives are found in the same proportions in the South as in the rest of the country. The shortage of Strong Liberals makes the South appear more conservative than it is. Fundamentalists are disproportionately represented only among Ordinary Conservatives and Bi-ideologicals.

Ordinary Liberals and Bi-ideologicals tend *not* to identify with the Middle Class. This means that if a message is explicitly addressed to the "Middle Class," many Ordinary Liberals and Bi-ideologicals would not know that the message was meant for them. It is the Strong Conservatives who are especially likely to identify with the Middle Class.

TABLE D.1 Demographic Uniqueness of Ideological Blocs

	Strong Liberal	Strong Conservative	Ordinary Liberal	Ordinary Conservative	Bi-ideological
Gender	Male +11				Female +10
Age	18–39 +11 Over 65 −10	18–39 −13	18–39 +18	18–39 −11 Over 65 +10	
Education	HS grad or less −14 College grad or more + 19	HS grad or less −13 College grad or more +12			HS grad or less +21 College grad or more −18
Race	While +11	White +21	Black and Hispanic +19		Black and Hispanic +24
Region	South −15				South +19
Income		>30,000 −17 <100,000 +14	>30,000 +13		>30,000 +23 <100,000 −17
Stockholder		Own stock +21	Own stock −17		Own stock −26
Religion	Fundamentalist −20 Protestant −13 Secular +30			Fundamentalist +17 Secular −13	Fundamentalist +17 Secular −12
Attend church	Never +32			Every week +12	Every week +12
Class Identification		Middle class +16	Middle class −10		Middle class −13

REFERENCES

Study	Principle Investigators
1960 ANES Time Series	Angus Campbell Philip Converse Warren Miller Donald Stokes
1964 ANES Time Series	Political Behavior Program
1968 ANES Time Series	Political Behavior Program
1972 ANES Time Series	Warren E. Miller Arthur H. Miller
1976 ANES Time Series	Warren E. Miller Arthur H. Miller
1980 ANES Time Series	Warren E. Miller
1984 ANES Time Series	Warren E. Miller
1988 ANES Time Series	Warren E. Miller
1992 ANES Time Series	Warren E. Miller Donald R Kinder Steven J. Rosenstone
1996 ANES Time Series	Warren E. Miller Donald R. Kinder Steven J. Rosenstone

2000 ANES Time Series	Nancy Burns
	Donald R. Kinder
	Steven J. Rosenstone
	Virginia Sapiro
2004 ANES Time Series	Nancy Burns
	Donald R. Kinder
2008 ANES Time Series	Jon A. Krosnick
	Arthur Lupia
2012 ANES Time Series	Vincent Hutchings
	Gary M. Segura
	Simon Jackman
2016 ANES Time Series	Vincent Hutchings
	Gary M. Segura
	Simon Jackman
	Shanto Iyengar
	Ted Brader

INDEX OF ELECTION CAMPAIGNS

INDEX OF CANDIDATE PROFILES

INDEX

Note: Page numbers followed by "n" denote endnotes.